Sugarhouse

* * *A Memoir* * *

MATTHEW BATT

MARINER BOOKS
A Mariner Original
Houghton Mifflin Harcourt
Boston   New York   2012

For information about permission to reproduce selections
from this book, write to Permissions, Houghton Mifflin Harcourt
Publishing Company, 215 Park Avenue South, New York, New York 10003.

WWW.HMHBOOKS.COM

Library of Congress Cataloging-in-Publication Data
Batt, Matthew
Sugarhouse: a memoir / Matthew C. Batt.
p. cm.
ISBN 978-0-547-63453-1 (pbk.)
1. Batt, Matthew C. — Homes and haunts — Utah —
Salt Lake City. 2. Dwellings — Maintenance and repair.
3. Batt, Matthew C. — Family. 4. Authors, American —
21st century — Biography. 5. Life change events. I. Title.
PS3602.A8977Z46 2012
818'.603 — dc23   2011028553

Book design by Patrick Barry
Printed in the United States of America

DOC 10 9 8 7 6 5 4 3 2 1

For Jeanne, Jenae, and Patti

Books and houses are a lot like piñatas. You never really know what you're going to find inside until you hit them with a stick. Or, of course, start reading about their ingredients. Most piñatas, you'll learn, are filled with real things like hard candy or jelly beans, but sometimes there are imitation things — like little erasers in the shape of jalapeños. Much less often, rutabagas. Inside this book are some sweet and some savory things, almost all of which are real. A few of them, however, are more eraser than jalapeño. That is, I had to change a few names and details to protect the more-or-less innocent. The following are pseudonyms: Stanley, Saul, Emma, Fiona, Tonya, and Daphne. The street name Franklin is also a pseudonym. Now then, here's your stick. Start swinging.

✳ CONTENTS ✳

1

It is a dreadful thing for the inhabitants
of a house not to know how it is made.

— RISTORO D'AREZZO, 1282

What We'll Call Home

YOU'VE SEEN US. *Them.* You've said to your sugar, What the hell do they think they're doing? You're on your stoop, your porch, your lanai, your whatever—and as we pass by you scrunch forward, down to car-window height. I'm gonna say something, you say, handing your honey the hose. Can't have people just driving around like that, all slow and everything, *rubbernecking.* Can I help you? you ask. You shake your head as we speed away. *Freaks.*

But you're just going to have to deal with it. We're not burglars or pedophiles, missionaries or Hari Krishnas. We're looking for a place to live. We need a home and we need one now.

It's the middle of July already, and it's a desert wasteland here in Salt Lake City. For eight days running it's been over a hundred degrees and the blacktop roads have begun to liquefy—not to mention this three-year drought that a thousand inches of rain won't fix. The air is so hot and brittle it feels as though my skin might shatter, and beyond that the lease on our apartment is up in six weeks and we just can't rent again. Jenae and I have been together for six years and have lived in nearly as many apartments. And it's not that Utah is exactly what we imagine when we say we want a place to call home, but it'll have to do for now. Still, we have no mover, no moving date, no home loan for that matter, and no home upon which we can make an offer.

It is not, however, for a lack of looking. Since May, Jenae (sounds like Renee with a J, as she says) and I have picked up every home-buyers' guide in the grocery store, studied each realty website till our eyes bled, and cased favorable neighborhoods so methodically we could put them back together from memory were they ever to fall apart. Then again, we've been driving around in Jenae's VW Beetle, a yellow poppy waving like a drag queen from the dash-board vase; we are a threat only to good sense, fundamentalists, and long-legged passengers.

Having rented apartments for so long, we usually lived near other renters. We met in Boston, where everybody we knew — rich or poor, young or old — lived in apartments, even if they owned them. In the West, and especially Utah, practically everyone we know owns her own house. Fellow waiters, writers, graduate students . . . everybody. Having just moved there, it made us feel like pariahs. It wasn't only how we paid for the roof above us, it was who we were and what we did to our communities: we were *renters*. An easy mark for the missionaries, for that matter.

When looking for an apartment, we had sought convenience, proximity to bars and grocery stores, off-street parking, sound-proofing against the klezmer music that wafted around our in-variably bohemian neighborhoods, a backyard for the beer-can bowling, a porch for the rocking chairs, and a nice corner for the spittoon. We didn't have to worry about the neighborhood, the neighbors, not even the place itself. It would have been like worry-ing about the feng shui of a bus station bathroom stall. An apart-ment is utilitarian and temporary. Go ahead, dance with that glass of red wine, smoke those cigars, fry up some catfish, juggle those skunks. You don't *live* here. You just rent.

To buy a house — or at least to look in earnest for one — is to admit to yourself that you think you're ready. At the very least, that you should be ready. Time to suck it up and recognize that there's relatively little pride to be had in the fact that your downstairs neighbors are as careful as they promise about cleaning their guns or that you managed to keep a ficus alive from Halloween until Thanksgiving, whereupon it shrugged all its leaves ceremonially to the floor. You're married, you're getting older, and your parents are looking more and more like the grandparents they are pestering you to make them. It's getting embarrassing. Your pathetic renter's mailbox — the one with three former tenants' names crossed out — is stuffed with your friends' baby-shower invitations. Just a few months ago, right after my grandmother died, five different people mentioned the word "ultrasound" to me on the same day.

There's something dreadful, however, about buying a house. You have to be willing to say to yourself, There go my freewheeling days of touring the Arctic on a kite-powered bobsled. So much for starting up that punk-rock band that was finally going to answer The Clash's call. If I'm hiking the Appalachian Trail, it's going to be with a Baby Bjorn or not at all. K2 and Kathmandu will have to take a bid on somebody else's death wish. I'm getting old. Forty might be the new thirty, but nobody who's twenty thinks so. It was time to grow up and settle down.

And, adulthood had just coldcocked us. First my adoptive dad died. Then Gram. Then Jenae's grandfather. These losses were devastating in their own ways, but Gram — her death was utterly unacceptable. All bets were off after that. Our best couple-friends were getting divorced. Doctors detected a strange mass in my mother's abdomen, and, not to be upstaged, my grandfather started having trouble with — among a raft of other things — his colon. It all seemed to be happening at the same time, on the same day, every hour on the hour.

Between the birth announcements and the death certificates, we couldn't tell up from down. Even the simplest facts and dates became obscured, irrelevant. All we knew was that everyone but us was dying, getting divorced, or having a kid, and we were stuck with our hands in our pockets waiting for the band to start. Life and death were coming for us, and we could either dig in, settle down, and try to defend the home front, or agree to shake hands and walk quietly away from the line and go our separate ways.

True, Utah seemed the oddest of places for us to be buying a house, but I was in a graduate program at the university and Jenae had recently landed a good job at a theater downtown, and since Gram had died, there was nothing to pull us back to the Midwest. Gram had been fading rapidly with Alzheimer's when I was admitted to the program, but she was perfectly clear when she threatened me if I quit school to move home. "Don't you dare," she said, clamping down on my hand like a pipefitter. "So help me God, I'll kill you myself."

I didn't want to stay in Utah, but I knew Gram could hold her liquor as well as she could throw a punch, and I just couldn't let her down. If we left Utah and the grad program I was in, it all would have been wasted and I'd be waiting tables full time. The long and the short of it was I was her only grandchild and she wanted me to make something of myself. That drive and her daughter's life were all she held on to all those years. After she died, it was time to act.

I had tried to defer settling down, kept telling Jenae and myself, *After I finish my master's.* And then, *Well, we can't buy a house on* an adjunct's salary, I better go back and get another degree. And then, Clearly we can't buy a house on a student's stipend. It was always something. Renting, like long-term dating or being a grad student or a waiter, is at once pathetic and comforting. You have announced to the world that you simultaneously aspire to grow up and move out of your childhood bedroom — your Michael Jackson *Thriller!* poster having been first hot, then sad, then ironic, then hot again, and then, finally, creepy and tragic — but you're not yet ready to be on your own.

We didn't want to be those people.

We began driving around and around, blowing off parties, leaving work early, eating nuclear things from the 7-Eleven, spiraling around greater Salt Lake City in our neo-retro car. The dashboard was littered with website printouts, pamphlets, for-sale-by-owner flyers, burrito wrappers, cigarette papers, ashes. Soon we felt like those dizzy, singed birds in that Yeats poem who can't find their way home and accidentally trigger the apocalypse. There was no telling. Jenae's car was a diesel Beetle and put out some fairly chunky exhaust.

Every For Sale sign we passed presented a philosophical, theological, existential quandary vis-à-vis geography. It was in the air in Salt Lake City, the spot where Brigham Young and his fiercely oh-so-sober band of true believers succinctly if unpoetically proclaimed, after years of wayfaring, "This is the place." Really. They did. There's even a This Is The Place Park, right by the university at the base of Emigration Canyon. Utah's a beautiful if somewhat literal-minded state.

So, a spit of arguably fertile land shimmed between a desert and a mountain. What does it mean to call this place home? Not for Brig, for us. How, after all, do we know if it *is* home? How many years, decades, or generations have to pass before we can say our brood calls this place home? Our friends back east would surely mock a Utah return address without an apartment number. Maybe we could get a post office box in Colorado, have the mail forwarded. Do we have to say we live here? Isn't it complicated enough to say, simply, we live?

Moreover, how will we decide on an actual house? Will we know it when we see it? Will we be able to say, This is the threshold I want to cross into the world every day. This is the lawn I'll hopelessly gird up for August. This the window the neighbor boy will break with his errant fly ball. This the tree from which the cat will learn to fly. The backyard where the spaniel will finally trump the squirrel. The kitchen where we'll burn sacrificial birds for our family's Thanksgiving. The office where I'll get some work done. The stoop where we can sit and share anything. The bedroom where we'll play God. The roof I'll stand on, defiant, garden hose in hand, watering the shingles against some wildfire. The front door we'll swing open, keys jingling from the lock, hollering like husbands, like wives, like fathers, like mothers, like those who own the thresholds they cross, Honey, I'm home!

Is this the place? Are *we* the people?

The Scene and the Scenery

JENAE AND I met in graduate school in Boston. Neither of us really knew what we were doing there. It was graduate school. School for graduates. Even the phrase implied we were doing something we had already done. We didn't know what we wanted out of it, just that we didn't want lifedom proper to officially start.

Initially I wore a blazer and glasses to class, even though I didn't really need either of them. My thermostat runs hot and my eyes were fine, but I had seen pictures of the Kennedys; I was doing what I thought I had to. Jenae arrived in Boston straight from Nebraska, sight unseen, with a couple hundred dollars, no place to live, and nothing — no shit — but a duffle bag over her shoulder. She was a pioneer in reverse. She was astonishing. I immediately noticed three things about her: (1) she did what she wanted, (2) she said what she thought, and (3) she wore really short skirts. I don't know that I'd call this feminism of the purest order, but something like it.

The first day of class, I sat next to her. Paul, our professor, had us arranged in a circle. The whole group soon devolved into a brutal argument about the nature of communication and the dim prospect of anyone actually knowing anyone else. To prove this point, Jenae and I disagreed violently with each other. The next class, I sat across from her. And not because of her skirt. I was so irritated and bothered, but also helplessly smitten, I felt like I was sitting on broken glass. She was the most contemptible, contrary, downright ornery woman I'd ever met. I'd seen *Casablanca*. I knew what that meant. I was *in* for it.

All the new students were invited to attend an informative gathering with something called The Bridge. At first I wondered if it wasn't some pre-AA thing for those of us seeking a way out of the beer-and-vomit-soaked undergraduate days. It turned out to be a student-run, nonprofit theater company made up almost exclusively of transplanted flatlanders, and it put on overlooked works of well-known writers. Guaranteed obscurity, in other words.

Despite my social awkwardness and complete lack of theater experience, I auditioned for and got the part of Duff in Harold Pinter's *Moonlight*. I think my casting had more to do with the likelihood of my being able to grow a mustache by the show date than histrionic promise, but who knows. The mid-nineties, at any rate, were not a grand time for twenty-two-year-old mustachioed men in greater Boston. I looked like that washed-up, back-from-the-Yankees scourge Wade Boggs. Not a welcome sight in the shadow of Fenway where I lived. But it was all for art, I told myself.

When the day of the show came, my joints went to jelly. I rode the T with my mustache and Irish tweed cap and vest, clenching my unlit pipe as if my virginity depended on it. When I got to campus the theater was awry with the whine of power tools and the smell of wet paint.

Just then a girl in overalls, a goofy bucket hat, and pigtails came up to me. She held a paintbrush in one hand and with the other grabbed my arm and whispered something supportive. Her hand — I thought it was mineral spirits — her hand *burned* my arm. I had never been held quite so firmly or so hotly. It was Jenae. From school. She was working with The Bridge? She seemed so different outside of the classroom. She stood there. She smiled. She held my arm. Lordy.

"I think I'm supposed to say 'break a leg,'" she said, her words like subtitles of a sweet silent film. Power saws sparked in the background and the lighting rig rose right over our heads.

I was vaguely dating a severely pale Connecticut girl who lived in an apartment where Edgar Allan Poe once vomited, and Jenae was going with a guy who had purportedly gotten her to eat steamed mussels on an early date. I told myself that that mattered. That we were in relationships.

"So," she said, "break a leg."

"Thanks," I said. "I just might."

My Fenway apartment cost $750 a month, as much as the lease on a Maserati in those days, but the kitchen was so small that you couldn't open the oven if the refrigerator was ajar, and when you were in the bathroom you had to be in the tub or on the toilet before you could shut the door. But on summer afternoons I could hear the organist at the ballpark practicing everything from "Take Me Out to the Ballgame" to "Blitzkrieg Bop." The Museum of Fine Arts was a five-minute walk across the Fens, and sometimes I'd go just to look at this one Hopper painting, *Room in Brooklyn,* which made me feel as if I were peering into a mirror that transformed me, awkwardly, into a mopey girl who sat around in her underwear waiting for something to happen. I was living alone for the first time and, for the most part, loved it, but I was also more lonely than I had ever imagined I could be. I only had classes a couple of times a week, and play rehearsals were infrequent. That left acres of time and space between me and the next human contact I'd have. If I didn't count clerks, bus drivers, and panhandlers, I could go for days without talking to or touching anyone.

Down my block was a bar and grill called Thornton's. It was owned by two Michigander brothers, Bud and Marty, and they gave me a job as a busboy and paid me in cash. They wore ponytails, T-shirts promoting tequila or light beer, and silver-tipped cowboy boots. If there was a God in Bud and Marty's universe, it was Bob Seeger and the Silver Bullet Band, and they tried to persuade their bartender Rock, an Iggy Pop stunt double who controlled the stereo, to play the great B.S. and the S.B.B. at least once a day. All of their sandwiches were named after Jack Nicholson movies or Grateful Dead trivia. Jerry's Missing Fingers, for example, being the least popular, if most intriguing.

Jenae, I learned, was paying $350 to share an apartment with a girl named Stacey, from Ishpeming, Michigan, and a forty-year-old finance guy from Framingham, Mass., who followed them from room to room turning the lights off to save money. This was in Jamaica Plain, a neighborhood where shop signs were in English, Irish, or Spanish.

The Bridge people hung out fairly often at the Brendan Behan, just down the hill from her apartment. From the outside, it was a prototypical black-and-gold-lettered Irish pub where you imagined there would be a fiddler and a tin-whistler and somebody in a burly sweater beating on the old tam, but once you opened the door you were nearly leveled by the sound and smoke. The place was tight and loud, and it felt as if you were trapped in the hold of a submarine working its way through a barrage of depth charges. We'd scream over the Fugazi or 7 Seconds about what a genius/prick James Joyce was and whether Samuel Beckett would have written for *Sesame Street* or *The Electric Company* if he were alive today. A pint of Guinness at the Behan would set you back six bucks, so we tried to stretch things out by drinking on an empty stomach or after donating blood.

"It's coming down to quitting drinking or selling plasma," Jenae said, looking balefully at the bottom of her empty glass.

I told her about Thornton's and how, after work, everybody got a free "shift beer," which often turned into a six-pack, so long as it wasn't anything fancy. She was intrigued. She had worked in, of all the world's mysteries, a seafood restaurant in Nebraska.

The next day, I asked Bud if they needed any more help.

"Is she hot?" he asked.

I blushed, said I guessed so.

"Tell her she can start tomorrow," Bud said. "But she better be hot."

After class let out one day, the rain caught us both. I asked Jenae how she was getting back to Jamaica Plain.

"I haven't melted yet," she said, unlocking her bike by the door.

"I — " I said. I had to use one hand to keep the other from trembling. She hadn't yet started at the restaurant, so we still hadn't spent much time with each other. "I could give you a ride?"

"I bet you could," Jenae said. "But I've got my bike."

I told her I had a bike rack. It was true, but it felt like a line anyway.

"Do you know how to use it?"

"I — " I said. I almost threw up.

"You're sweet," she said, putting her helmet on. "But I'm meeting Stacey. We ride home together."

I did some quick calculating.

"It's a two-bike bike rack," I said.

When I pulled up to their skinny building, which was shingled in tarpaper made to look like bricks, Stacey hopped out first.

"You ought to stay for a while," she said. "It's Wednesday. Root beer float day."

"I don't like owing people anything," Jenae said. "This is probably a long way for you."

I told her not at all, even though I was so lost I was probably going to have to hire a taxi to follow back to Fenway — I had only ever taken the T out there, and the roads were strewn about between here and there like a pot of spilled noodles.

"How about this," she said. She pulled a strand of hair from her lips. "You come up for a root beer float and we'll call it even."

"Deal," I said.

And it was.

We were soon spending upward of a hundred hours a week together, slinging burgers during the lunch shift around Fenway, dozing through classes in the afternoons, fumbling through play rehearsals in the evenings, and then pounding clam chowder out of bread boules at Doyle's or Guinness at the Behan, fighting over Heaney and Yeats, playing darts till bar time at the Silhouette in Allston, whirling around greater Boston in a daze of heat, grease, beer, and shellfish. Pretty much before either of us knew what happened, there we were, a tangle of knees and elbows on my futon on Park Drive, the sun climbing up the Prudential Building before we even shut our eyes.

Suddenly it was August. We had acquired a puppy and had lived together for a year, and now we were packing a van at midnight to move to Columbus, Ohio. More grad school for me, and who knew what for Jenae.

I couldn't believe it. She was coming with me. We were actually a couple. I could hear Pinter, Yeats, and Hopper cheering us on from behind their lonely tapestries.

When most people would have felt around for a ladder or a rope, Jenae jumped. To leap from this clutch of artists, expert liars, and aspiring drinkers; from this town rich in history, fish and chips, and beer at any cost; from the first home away from home for both of us, newly settled in and barely explored, to . . . Columbus, the heralded meteorological groin of Ohio? If ever there was a brave explorer, I daresay it was not the namesake of our future hometown, but Jenae.

At first, of course, it was rough. The day we arrived, the sky was green between apocalyptic blasts of thunder and lightning, and the air gagged us with humidity. The rivers smelled sordid and flammable. People ate at White Castles, as though there were anything royal about steaming their hamburgers. This was going to take some getting used to.

Early on, a couple of guys in my grad school program took me to Mickey's Bar and I bought a round with a five-dollar bill and got change back, after the tip. And then I realized we were talking about writing. Not like in Boston, where all we could talk about were writers. We were shooting pool, wearing cheese-stained T-shirts, listening to George Thorogood slice through pantywaist indecision by ordering three drinks at once, and we were talking about writing. *Our* writing.

At Ohio State, my peer mentor was this burly, bighearted Texan named Bruce. We talked on the phone just once, and before we hung up he had arranged for Jenae and me and Maggie, our sweet, six-month-old English cocker spaniel, to stay at his apartment while we looked for one of our own. Even though he was going to be out of town. Even though we had never met.

Bruce quickly became the kind of friend to me that brothers rarely make for each other. A friend of his from Houston, "a poet," he warned, was entering my program too: a grizzly-bearded chain smoker named Bryan, who was as infamous for his iambs as he was his kilts. Though Bruce and Bryan were from Texas, they both had a strong proclivity for the North and all its trappings. Snow, pea coats, upland birds, dark beer, and soups, stews, and chowders for starters. Bryan, despite his most recent return address, was born in Cleveland, "by mistake," he insisted. And I, despite having lived most of my life in Wisconsin, was born in Denver, which, granted, didn't make me an obvious member of their clan. Then I met Bruce's father, Allen, who showed me an 1845 map of the Republic of Texas — the only one a true Texan would abide. According to the map, where the panhandle shoots up clear through Colorado and even into some of unsuspecting Wyoming, I was a northern Texan, but a Texan nonetheless. Somehow or other we were all fellow expatriates and found ourselves, more often than not, smoking, grilling, swilling, and prevaricating on Bruce's stoop on 6th Avenue. We were as unlikely as unreasonably good friends.

Bruce was married to an Arkansan named Emma, who seemed to follow whoever was cooking and scrub behind them as though salmonella were predatory. She did something with computers for which people flew her all over and paid her a lot of money. Their ebullient apricot-and-white Brittany, named Irma Jean, could bounce high enough to lick your teeth and liked to lounge on the back of their sofa as though it were the instrument she was born to master. Bryan was married to Sarah, a social worker from Denver, who had the patience of a glacier and needed every cube of it, given Bryan's demeanor, which was as surly as it was sweet. Their cocker, named Cordwainer (aka Bubba), could sniff out a bagel in a safe and flattered me by peeing on no one's shoes but mine.

Jenae was working at the Columbus AIDS Task Force, which was as meaningful a place to work as it was physically and emotionally exhausting. The fact that Bruce and Bryan and I were great friends and grad student idlers and that Jenae and Sarah and Emma had real jobs and didn't have all the time that we did to coalesce as friends, things were a little cockeyed, but I was happier than I had ever been in my life.

After the afternoon workshops technically ended, classes would migrate across High Street to Larry's Bar & Seminar, as it was called, for pitchers of swampy Molson Golden, baskets of chile-dusted peanuts, and the even straighter take on the shop talk that night. I got home from "class" one night, four pitchers to the wind, with bits of peanut shell stuck between my teeth, to find Jenae tear-streaked and furious.

"Hey," I tried, "baby?"

"Whatever," she said.

Wow. I realized I was being a complete asshole. We were having a great time when we were all together, but when we weren't, I was in my own little world.

One autumn day not long after that, I found myself golfing with Lee Abbott. It sounds pretentious — golfing with the great author! — but students could make tee times at the OSU championship courses, whereas faculty had to be members. Lee would have golfed with Idi Amin if it meant getting a tee time.

It was a nautical kind of day, around forty degrees, the wind gusting the flag sticks close to parallel with the ground, the rain right on the border of hail, but neither of us would admit that it was a stupid day to be anywhere but a bar. We both struck sufficiently good drives down a long par four, and as we sloshed down the fairway, he lit philosophically one of his Red 100s.

"Matt, my boy," he said, "you have dragged this woman of yours all over creation, have you not?"

We hadn't even been talking about Jenae, but I told him that he was pretty much right, so long as the distance between Boston and Columbus could be construed as "creation."

"I am not," he said, tapping ashes, "interested in frivolity, dillydallying, or shilly-shallying."

We stopped at his ball, nicely laid up just shy of a sand trap. He pulled out El Conquistador, his trusty lob wedge.

"When are you going to do right by that woman?" he asked, flicking his cigarette to the turf. "Time to propose or get off the pot, am I right?"

He didn't need to look me in the eye for me to know it wasn't an idle question. He chipped his ball right up to the flagstick.

Jenae and I had been living together for three years by then. We were dog-parents together. We knew how to fold each other's laundry. We'd go on "condom raids" with her friends at the local gay bars and to poetry readings in brewpubs with mine. We'd order nachos and a burger and split them as though it were second nature. We knew what kind of beer to order if the other was in the bathroom. I had thought it beside the point to have some ceremony and get a new set of titles. Being boyfriend/girlfriend seemed to have it all over husband/wife. As Billy Bragg says, doesn't marriage just prove that our parents were right? Isn't it the first step in getting divorced?

But we were in love — really, truly, deeply — and I wanted to marry that girl. Lee knew that. My mom knew that. And my grandma, who grew up on a farm and knew what it meant to have to walk a field of beans just like Jenae did, positively adored her. I hadn't looked forward to getting married in the abstract, but all the particulars told me to do otherwise. And Bruce and Emma, Bryan and Sarah — all my favorite people were married, I realized. I wanted us to be them. I wanted us *all* to get married.

Economy

TO AUGMENT MY grad student stipend of four dollars a semester, I work at a Salt Lake City restaurant called, of all things, The New Yorker, and between shifts and school I cruise around Sugarhouse, one of two viable neighborhoods for liberal types who want to live in Utah but pretend they're still in America. I'm on my hazard-orange Vespa-ish scooter, wearing waiter's clothes, carrying a messenger bag loaded with flyers, a notebook, and — honest to God — *Moby Dick*.

I believe in accidents. Generally not the kind that will lay me out on the pavement, but rather the kind where I'll turn a corner Jenae and I have turned a thousand times in her VW, and because I'm not in the Bug but on the vehicular equivalent of a T-ball stand, and therefore extra-careful about entering the flow of traffic, I might just see something I wouldn't have seen before. A lime-green-jacketed realtor digging a hole for a new post, an appraiser down the street tape-measuring the yard, or the type of little red and white sign you buy at a hardware store to put on the dashboard of your life-size Camaro lawn ornament.

One blistering afternoon I notice a small, mustachioed man watering the lawn in the middle of the day — in the middle of a drought — in the middle of a desert! He seems more like a capricious landlord or sociopathic golf course groundskeeper than a homeowner. From what I can see, there's no furniture inside and nothing on the walls. Only a ladder in the kitchen and a bucket of paint on the countertop.

It's a house we've seen before. The cream-colored masonry caught my eye; it reminded me of the kind of brick they built everything with in Milwaukee, my more-or-less hometown. It's got double-hung windows with huge stone casements and a big, fenced-in backyard with a haggard rose bush in the front, big as a small tree. The street name, Franklin, feels as full of promise as the Constitution itself.

It's on the corner of the street Jenae and I have come to call our favorite in Sugarhouse: 800 East, a quiet, straight haven of pavement between two of the busiest roads in Salt Lake. Wide enough for parking on both sides, but narrow enough so that only ten-speeds or Big Wheels drag race here. It's one of the few neighborhoods in all of Salt Lake where the streets have not just numbers and letters but names, like Browning and Emerson — poets and writers, no less. The homes are set back a fair bit from the road, but not so far that you can't hear your neighbor when he *Hulloes!* to you in the morning. Any hour of the day you'll find strollers, joggers, bikers, dog walkers, unicyclists, roller skaters, speed walkers, kite flyers, bums, drunks, missionaries, cops, robbers, cowboys, Indians . . . every day, the hoi polloi on parade under a thatchwork canopy of oaks older than all of us put together.

Although 8th East, as it's called, is not exactly on my way to or from anything, I had forced myself to take it as often as possible, having quickly learned that real estate, even in a supposed buyer's market, can come and go in a day without so much fanfare as a SOLD sticker.

A few days later, when I see the red and white For Sale sign in the window of that house on 8th, I can't help but feel like Ahab. Not the peg-legged one who nailed a gold doubloon to the mast, all cocksure and blustery, but the one who must have about choked on his hardtack every time some bloody fool atop the mizzenmast shouted, *Thar she blows!* only to have spotted another right or blue or goddamned Greenland whale and not the mighty sperm that was his Moby Dick.

But there it is, finally, on this scorching day in July: a sign — a *sign!* — in the window. This must be the place.

I park my scooter, drop my helmet on the seat, and run up to the door. I call the number on my cell phone as I peer inside. The phone rings and rings, and it begins to sound more like the distant alarm I'm feeling. The house, from what I can see, is disgusting. If this is going to be The House, I think, it's going to start out like Cinderella's story wherein we will be forced to spend a lot of painful time on our hands and knees at the behest of a cruel stepmother, waiting for something magical to happen with wands, a squash, geriatric fairies, and rodents.

A man's small, pinched voice comes through the line, and it is not, I realize, my fairy godmother. I tell him who I am, why I'm calling, where I'm calling from.

He sounds as if he's ready to be highly annoyed with me, as if he were expecting a federal agent or property appraiser. When he understands that I might give him money rather than pinch it, he chippers up.

"I can be there in half an hour. Half an hour. I'll hurry hurry. Just down here in Murray, you know. Be there right quick. We'll show you the place, we will all right. Name's Stanley, by the way," he says. "Stanley. See you soon."

I scoot to a convenience store, buy a Coke, and zip back to the house, hoping the glare of the window was playing tricks on my eyes. I look inside again and think about calling my landlord to see about extending our lease. Thank God my grandmother isn't around to see this. The apparent condition of the house seethes from between the bricks. If it were a person, I would recommend, if not dramatic surgery, a generously cut caftan and a personal trainer or two. A burka perhaps.

I call Jenae at work, who's guarded but optimistic, and then Sully, our last-chance realtor. In his jaded, realtor way, Sully is piqued. He knows from experience that we have been nearing the Fuck It stage of home buying. It is preceded by the Just Looking stage, the Very Interested stage, the We Love It We'll Take It stage, the What Do You Mean Our Offer Fell Through? stage, then the Well This Is the One We Really Liked Anyway stage, followed by the It's Already Under Contract? stage, and finally, of course, the Fuck It stage, when exasperation courts thirty-year (or, hell, even adjustable-rate) mortgages with all the grace and romance involved in asking your cellmate if he'll rub lotion on your back.

"So," Sully says, "you found another one. Super!" He seems campily amused by the fact that every house I have found has fallen through. As if he has been blameless by finding and showing us house after house that we hate. "And you said it's listed through who?"

I tell him it's for sale by owner, and Sully laughs.

"What?" I say. I am not amused. My grandmother is three months dead, and my mother has been a listing wreck, sick with grief. I am working two jobs, we are still broke, about to become homeless, and it is over a hundred freaking degrees for the eighth day in a row. People have shot strangers for less.

"What, Sully?" I say.

"Nothing," Sully says. I can hear him leaning back like an executive, even though he is a waiter with me at the restaurant more often than he is a businessman. Mostly he's a really good guy, but now is not the time. "Just gotta love the Fisbos," he says.

"The whats?"

"The Fisbos. For Sale by Owners. They're all just — well, you'll see."

I sit on the porch, smoke a cigarette, and wonder what in God's name I am waiting for, momentarily confusing Fisbo with Furby, that undead, self-animated stuffed thing with a beak, when a white Dodge Diplomat with imitation wood paneling and Idaho plates pulls up. It is the kind of car driven by, I imagine, someone who has a cellar full of Spam, Fanta, guns, and ammunition. Maybe even a cache of armor-piercing rounds for the big day when the feds try their Ruby Ridge routine again. The car's license plate appears to be attached to the rear bumper with a coat hanger. A man wearing a white T-shirt and jean shorts gets out. His shorts are so short that one pocket hangs below the ragged hem, and I worry for a moment that it's not his pocket.

"You must be Stanley," I say.

I stand up somewhat awkwardly, realizing I'm on his porch, greeting the owner of the house as if he were me, someone I have been waiting for so I can sell him this damned house. He walks directly toward me at near-ramming speed, then stops abruptly, squares up, and shakes my hand. His fingers are callused and meaty, like thick-skinned sausages, and to him my unmanly hand probably feels like a warm, soggy croissant.

"Hi," he says. "How are ya?"

I say okay.

"Well," he says, taking the key from his floppy pocket, "let's get you on the grand tour."

As soon as he opens the door, the smell hits me — something between a derelict litter box, muddy diapers, and a basement backed up with wastewater — and my eyes begin to tear as I crane my head around for one last breath.

"Lady used to live here," Stanley says, happy as a man without a nose, "she had a cat or two."

It reeks like a state fair Porta Potty during a heat spell and a sanitation strike. I check to see if my nose is bleeding. Stanley, I'm thinking, must have smelling salts nestled into his little mustache.

Stanley reminds me of the superintendent of the apartment building where I lived in Boston. His name was also Stanley. Stanley the super single-handedly taught me everything I needed to know about that peculiar Massachusetts accent. Whenever you greet someone, whether you know him or not, like or hate him, you say, all as one word, "Hihowahya." At first I thought it was, perhaps, a traditional Penobscot Indian salutation, a terse but well-meant expression of welcome to weary travelers. But no. It's the classic New England question-that-is-not-a-question.

I keep my mouth shut for pretty much the whole tour and try to breathe through my T-shirt when Stanley isn't looking. I needn't let the smell distract me from the fact that I don't know a thing about what to look for in a house. Hell, my wife and I have bought cars because of their cup holders, the synecdochic equivalent of buying a house because it has a nice mailbox. Which this one does not. It has a rusted metal thing screwed into the mortar by the front door. In a previous life it may have been a cracker tin.

Stanley is a sharp judge of character. At the same time, I am not very hard to read. A crazy-haired, scooter-riding, table-waiting kid who apparently has some kind of delivery to make. Not an obvious choice for anything but debt and regret. So while I look around and nod and struggle with the might of olfaction, Stanley tells me the story of his house the way he might to someone with a hearing aid or conspicuous frontal lobe damage.

"Last lady, she was just a renter. Rent the place for ten years or so. Never caused any trouble. One kid, ugly but quiet. No complaints. Had the HUD people come out, do a little insulation stuff, you know, to keep the bills down, but she was a good woman. Paid the rent on time."

He turns toward me, but he doesn't like to stand face-to-face. I notice that as I pivot toward him, he pivots away, as though it's important to him that we are constantly looking not at each other but in the same direction.

"Neighbors'll tell you she sold the crack cocaine — the windows was all shut up with foil and cardboard. But don't you listen to that horse hockey."

I'm not sure what that means or why he's telling me. He is a strange man.

"Lady liked her privacy is all. Her kid used to bury his dolls in the yard. Not much to say about that."

We're standing in the foyer. The walls are white. A shiny, hard, automotive white that would cover up nearly any kind of bad news from the past. For a while, anyway. The ceilings are high, and that's an unmitigated plus, but the floors — they're covered by carpets that look and smell like the oily, seepy mud revealed at low tide in industrial ports. At any time I imagine we could come across hypodermic needles, charred spoons, crack vials, spare tires, once-troublesome union organizers.

"Anyway, before that," Stanley continues, "the wife and I lived in it up until we had kids, and before that, my mother and dad lived in it, and before that, my grandparents. They built it their own selves in 1911. Been in the family the whole time," he says distractedly, perhaps thinking of where to put one more room deodorizer.

I get the feeling he goes through this spiel on a fairly regular basis, which is odd because I could have sworn he just put it up for sale. I might be getting to the point in the tour when the majority of prospective buyers succumb to nasal attrition.

He nods through a doorway to the living room. It has the same septic aura about it, but I keep telling myself that they're both big rooms with tall, nine- or ten-foot ceilings. The one has a large, south-facing picture window, the other has one too, as well as a curving bay window on the east, through which you can see at least the idea of mountains.

As Stanley tries to tell me about how he was tired of having to keep up two properties and whatnot, I am trying to tell myself: Look at the light. Look at the windows. Look at the ceilings. Look at all the *room*. But all I can see or hear or think is the smell. To make matters worse, Renuzit Super Odor Killers sit in the corners of both rooms, adding an imitation-berry tinge to the stench. I expect to turn a corner and find a commode filled with week-old Thai food, rotting fruit, and bad clams.

By turning myself toward the kitchen, I square-dance Stanley out of the living room and away from the heart-of-darkness carpet. There is, however, little in the way of consolation to be found. The kitchen smells like rubber cement and burning fiberglass, and wood veneer covers the cabinets, the drawers, the walls — I'm sure the avocado refrigerator is next. There is a ladder against the wall, and it's just a matter of time before he gets around to paneling the ceiling.

An apartment Jenae and I briefly considered living in back in Ohio also had wall-to-wall carpet/litter box. When the landlord showed us around, doing the and-this-is-the-bathroom routine, he said, "And the cabinets are all knotty pine — if you're into that kind of thing." At the time, I didn't know if that was supposed to be funny or architecturally relevant. Then we saw it. What he meant wasn't just that a couple of cabinets were made of that cheap, unfinished, sadly shellacked wood full of eye-like knots ogling you from above. No, the whole kitchen was rendered in knotty pine. Knotty pine basin for the sink. Knotty pine pantry. Knotty pine faux shutters. Knotty pine breakfast nook. Knotty pine napkin cozy. Knotty pine pine-knot knobs for the knotty pine drawers.

But Stanley's house is a whole other level. At least that knotty pine in Ohio was actual wood. This paneling is a badly focused photograph of knotty pine printed on some plastic/cardboard abomination made from recycled Trapper Keepers and tampons.

Stanley is saying something about the work he is doing in the kitchen. On the yellow plastic counter sits a can of high-gloss white paint, a coffee can of rusty bolts and screws, and a few strips of used imitation wood molding.

"I know it doesn't look that great on the surface," Stanley says, my sudden confidant, "but that's what the women are good at — the little touches." He pronounces "women" as though it had two *i*'s in it: wimin. I know it's wrong, but I kind of like it.

"How long you plan on being here?"

The question catches me off-guard. "Probably five years," I guess. I haven't thought about it. I don't know if there's a right answer or not. I can't imagine anybody would refuse to sell a house to someone because he didn't think the buyers were going to be in it for the long haul, but anything seems possible with Stanley.

"See, then," Stanley says, "this here is perfect." His eyes narrow and he leans forward conspiratorially. He twitches his little dust-broom mustache, and I'm afraid it's time for the secret Masonic handshake and Lord knows what else. "Lemme show you something," he says.

On the yellow plastic kitchen counter, under the rusty can of screws, is a stack of photocopies. They are, Stanley tells me, appraisals and listings of neighboring houses. "Lookit," he says, "they

put this house over on Browning at one-eighty-nine!" He back-
hands the paper as if it has told him a real boy-and-howdy of a
joke. "This one on Emerson, one-seventy-five! And look here,
they're the same as this house. Two bedrooms — okay, so this one
on Browning has got three — and one bath — well, the Browning
place has another half bath downstairs — but it's just a shitter on
the main drain. I can add a half bath in a jiffy if it's important to
you, but I'm telling you, in the basement they're no good for any
real work a toilet needs to do. Gotta get whatever you put in it
back up to street level. Anyway, beyond that, those properties are
exactly like this one."

Even on the poor photocopies I can see that the other houses
are far better tended — like bonsai trees managed by a fleet of the
emperor's gardeners compared to the haggard shrub of this house.
But somehow Stanley has got me hooked. Hooked but hopeless.
I feel I'm doing an advanced math problem, where x is the house
now and the solution is a complete renovation, with shiny floors,
cheerily painted walls, and a kitchen that could never be confused
with the current one — but I have no idea how to solve for y. My
homeowning ignorance at this point could not possibly be over-
stated, being, as it is, worse than my math metaphors.

The state of the house and the urgency of the market have para-
lyzed me. I'll mention this place to Jenae because, of course, we've
had our eye on it, but she won't have to go inside. She'll be able to
smell it from the curb — *cat piss! crack cocaine!* — and she'll kick
me out of the car and say something timeless like, "I don't even
know who you are anymore," and that will be that. You simply cannot profoundly disagree about the single biggest investment of
your life. Certainly not violently disagree, which is what I'm afraid
is in store.

Jenae has worked as, for, and with artists and designers. Her taste is as eclectic as it is impeccable, and her opinions are resolute in proportion to their individuality. You don't get to be the first woman to go to graduate school from practically your whole college by simpering and acquiescing. She likes what she likes and she is who she is. She's got Annie Hall's spunk and singularity, Katharine Hepburn's grit, grace, and determination, and, if pushed, Annie Oakley's quick draw and deadeye. She is not a person who does what you expect. And while I so love that about her, it also scares me. About this house, I don't rightly know what she'll think.

"I know it seems unbelievable," Stanley says, "but this house is worth a lot more money than I'm asking for. And until I get what I know is fair, I'll keep doing things myself that'll make it look better to the womenfolk. The way I see it, you buy it like it is, you get to finish up things the way you want, let the wife feel like she's in on it."

The air seems a little less putrid for a moment and I'm able to consider what he's saying, condescension aside. There is a kind of truth to it, I know. I just don't know what kind of truth, or whether it will have any purchase with Jenae.

"Look, I'll show you. You'll see for yourself. I redone all the plumbing, all the 'lectrical, even put a new roof on — new sheathing and all." He pauses to scratch his overly exposed, tapiocaed thigh. "Everything like that I done right. Pulled out all the old knob-and-tube wiring. Not just at the outlets, neither. All the way down the walls. Big pain in the keister, but I done it right."

The precious little I know about homeownership, picked up from friends and family, is that the things he just mentioned are the reasons people take out third mortgages and hire contractors who more or less end up moving in and selling the house themselves after they've bankrupted the owners.

I glance outside at Stanley's Diplomat. It has the same paneling as the cabinets. How can I not trust this man? Of what guile, what subterfuge, could a man like this be capable?

There is something about Stanley that reminds me, inexplicably, of Henry David Thoreau. They both fancy themselves intrepid homesteaders and handymen, and both are liable to be a little more than tedious when the tax man comes around. Accordingly, they thrive on being cheap, penny-pinching pariahs.

When Thoreau finished college (he didn't do particularly well), he dawdled around before settling into business with his father. Ralph Waldo Emerson, Thoreau's friend, neighbor, and part-time caterer while at his pond estate, wrote of this time: "His father was a manufacturer of lead pencils, and Henry applied himself for a time to this craft, believing he could make a better pencil than was then in use. After completing his experiments, he exhibited his work to chemists and artists in Boston, and having obtained their certificates to its excellence and to its quality with the best London manufacture, he returned home contented. His friends congratulated him that he had now opened his way to fortune. But he replied that he should never make another pencil. 'Why should I? I would not do again what I have done once.'"

Undistinguished academically, marginally employable, no trade under his belt, Thoreau seeks his father's wing only to essentially say: You've been doing this all your life, Dad, and you're a chump. I may not know a thing about writing instruments, but I do know a bad pencil when I see one, and that there is a bad pencil you're making. I'm going to make a better one.

And he does.

And then he quits.

Not because he couldn't have made a mint from it. Not because he didn't know its value. His whole goal was to prove he could achieve a higher standard by sheer will alone, and then, to prove how high and mighty his standard was, flush it.

If Thoreau were alive today, he might have pulled up to the house as Stanley did, driving a twenty-five-year-old station wagon. For all the trumpery and fanfare surrounding *Walden,* at the core of self-reliance and transcendentalism — and Thoreau himself — is ostentatious thrift and self-fashioned pride. Nothing makes him so proud as the fact that he has to work for only six weeks in order to butter his parsnips for the whole year.

Stanley leads me downstairs, and he's back to telling me about the work he's done, talking fast as a pencil sharpener. He's pointing to overhead pipes and wires and fuses and breakers, telling me about voltages and amperages and gallons per flush and the like. It all sounds right, and I can't imagine Stanley having the pistachios to flat out lie about that kind of stuff, but still. I have no real idea what he's talking about.

The dominant feature of the basement is a twin furnace that sits like a medium-size town's incinerator right in the middle of the floor. Ducts big as water slides go up in every direction and extend down from the ceiling every few feet, so you have to bend over and scoot around them. It looks like a small-time but earnest oil refinery. The ceiling itself is about six feet high — I notice that if I force myself to stand up straight and walk between ducts I can barely clear the beams. Stanley, a good foot shorter than me, walks around like Yoda in his swamp, not even ducking for the ducts as he points out his masterly plumbing and electrical work.

This is, in fact, one nasty-ass house, but I know that Stanley has a point and a purpose. Houses in urban markets get bought. It might take a few months, maybe a year, but they get bought. Who cares if a thousand people hate the house? Only one of them has to buy it.

Stanley, who has never paid a mortgage on this house and already has another, new one, is indifferent. He has a kind of placid arrogance about him, despite his unpolished sales patter and conspicuously blemished house. It's like the little card that comes with leather wallets: any imperfections in the material are guarantees of its authenticity. He didn't let it get to him that his house was as grungy as a thrift store dumpster — if it smelled or looked any better, it would show the world he cared more about its superficial life and not, say, the intrinsic beauty of a well-hung line of 15-amp electrical conduit.

On our way back to the kitchen, I notice that the trim around one window frame is pulling away from the plaster. When I tap it, a four-foot section of it peels right off and clatters to the floor. Stanley frowns, picks up the trim, and leans it up against the ladder.

"Glue ain't set is all," he says, irritated that I would trust him so little as to require evidence of his handiwork. "You don't gotta believe me, but everything'll be tip-top — whenever you want to move in. And you got to know, this house is worth a whole sight more than I'm asking."

"You think?" I say. I don't doubt him. But I feel he needs me to.

"I could easily get this house appraised higher — put in new carpet, lay another sheet of linoleum in the kitchen, put on some fancy new drawer pulls, all that garbage — but I just ain't interested. It'd raise the taxes, you know." Stanley winks conspiratorially at me, as if only he and I and his militia buddies know what property taxes are really for. "This lack of so-called taste — consider it my gift to you."

I know I am ignorant and a pushover, but I also know that something small and seed-like is hatching. There is no doubt as to why he is selling this house. A pair of corks and a tube of caulk couldn't keep the smell from you. The carpeted floors have a spongy, swamp-like feel underfoot. The kitchen looks to have been staged to induce Martha Stewart's hari-kari. The basement's low ducts and leviathan furnace are clearly capable of consuming the house, if not in flames, at least in gas bills. Time and money unfurl before the state of this place toward the vanishing point.

But if not to reinvent a space, to take what's present and see what's possible, to scour the sores and blights and paint the beauty and make it bloom — that's imagination, I'm thinking. Isn't that what we humans are here for, at least conceptually?

I have probably read too much transcendental literature for my own good, yet Stanley's warped but seductive logic has also begun to have its thrifty way with me. Then again, there might be something toxic and possibly narcotic still festering in the drywall or carpet.

"So," I say, "how soon will you be ready to sell?"

"Oh, any time, I expect. Only thing is," he says, trying poorly to conceal a wry grin, "there's this Oriental girl come by the other day."

We're in the kitchen again and he's leaning against the wood-veneered cabinets. He strokes the warped, brass-colored plastic trim on the counter. It is so obvious that he is messing with me. Just because Stanley uses recycled nails doesn't mean they don't have points on them. He can see his plan coming together, but not without a little value-added service.

"This woman?" he says. "She's real innerested. Even says she's got some ideas for putting a refrigerator in where these cabinets are. Came by and checked it out with a tape measure and everything." He shakes his head. "Oriental woman with a tape measure," he says. "What's next?"

Sounds like a beautiful, if racist, still life to me, but I don't have time to dwell on it.

He shows me out to the front porch and we shake hands as we did when we met, only now he's on the porch and I'm on the steps, and he's clearly selling, and I am clearly buying.

The Cuts and Clarities of Diamonds

SHE SAID *YES!*

I squeezed the nicest ring my credit card could accommodate and down I went on one knee. And when I got back up, we were engaged. The next summer, hitched we were, with Bruce and Emma, Bryan and Sarah among our wedding party. We were all so close they made our hometown friends and family seem like intruders. Bruce and Bryan got me — for real — a shotgun as a gift, but nobody needed it to motivate me that day. Jenae, radiant in a dress she made herself, walked down the aisle that hot August afternoon like my own sweet epiphany. To quote "Brown Penny," the Yeats poem we assigned a reluctant Bryan to read at the ceremony, I was "looped in the loops of her hair."

For a while, we were the happiest people we knew. Bruce and Emma, Bryan and Sarah, Jenae and I. We were having the time of our lives. Before long, Bryan and Sarah had a beautiful little son, and Bruce and Emma and Jenae and I were the godparents. He felt like our commune baby. It was ridiculous. All our sweet spaniels, and now a baby to boot.

It was such a joyous time, but not an infinite one. None of us could stay. Bryan got into a doctoral program in Missouri. Emma got into law school in Boston. Within three months they were all gone. Jenae and I were alone with each other — married to be sure, but stuck was what it felt like.

I got a job teaching an hour away, in Newark, Ohio, whose most prominent feature is the Longaberger headquarters, shaped like a sixteen-story picnic basket. Jenae quit the nonprofit to try her hand at fashion design, but the woman she worked for was as charming as a shiv and had an unfortunate tendency toward DUIs and bounced checks. We were both out of school, on our own, and not doing very well at being adults. We were drinking more, talking less. I began hiding myself in the attic, playing guitar, chain-smoking, and experimenting with facial hair. She got a rescue cat and cable TV and worked on a quilt for someone else's baby.

It wasn't so much that we were *un*happy. We just weren't *happy* happy as we'd been. When you don't have anything else to do but worry about whether you're happy or not, well, you do.

And then, just as we were circling our own drain, my dad was diagnosed with what looked to be double pneumonia.

I called him Dad, but he was my mom's second husband, twenty years her senior, nearly fifty years older than me. They married when I was seven, my biological father having been out of the picture practically from the moment I was born. My adoptive father fought in the Second World War and played big league baseball for the St. Louis Browns in the early fifties, and he still loved the game. He had developed type 2 diabetes and his eyesight was failing, so when I was a kid and we played catch on summer evenings he'd end up with bruises all over his stomach and chest.

Then, after he and my mom grew apart and themselves divorced,

I saw him only a few times a year, though he remained beatific in his kindness. To me, to Jenae (whose name he always remembered despite its eccentric spelling and his failing health), to everyone. When I went to Madison to visit him in the hospital, I realized I wouldn't be going back to Columbus until there was a funeral. I called Jenae, and without balking she got on the next flight.

When she arrived, Dad was basically unconscious, but he roused as though he'd only been taking a catnap. "Hey there, Jenae," he said. "Thanks for coming. You gotta be tired from traveling." He patted the bed next to him. "Come and sit down, sweetheart."

Throughout this time, I couldn't help but feel a bit like an outsider. After all, this was in Madison, where his daughters from his first marriage lived. They were all kind and generous with me, but they were also anywhere from fifteen to twenty-five years older than I was. And since they were sisters, they had their own language. Without Dad to bring me into the middle, I was lost.

Jenae ignored all that. She hugged and held everybody, wiped their snotty faces, pulled hair from their eyes, laughed at their runny makeup. She joked with their recalcitrant spouses and made their children feel cheeky and talented. She made us eat frozen custard and bought clean socks at a grocery store for everybody. She slept on the floor of Dad's hospice room, neither asking for nor needing permission, and she sat with me on his last night, holding my hand while I held his.

When we got back to Ohio, however, things felt empty. I hated where I was teaching. I had an hourlong commute, and had recently taken on a four-hour round-trip once a week to teach an extra class on business writing to inmates at a prison. Jenae had just

begun doing event management for a man who wore untrustwor-
thily tight pants. We needed something new, but we didn't know
what. Columbus had become as useful and beautiful as a swollen
appendix, and we needed to get out before something burst.

My grandparents had moved to Wisconsin to be closer to my
mom when my grandmother's health began to deteriorate. She
was suffering from Alzheimer's and a host of thyroid-related af-
flictions. They had only just finished building their dream house,
across the street from the country club in Pekin, when it became
apparent that they couldn't be four hours away from my mom. After they moved into their condo in Waukesha, five minutes from
my mom's place, Gram started to slip irrevocably away.

At the same time, during a routine checkup doctors found a
strange mass in my mom's abdomen and immediately scheduled
her for surgery. No one knew what to think or do, especially because she was so calm about it.

Meanwhile, I had applied to PhD programs in hopes of making
something substantive happen with my career. Jenae was reasonably opposed. She was afraid that I would devolve again, leaving
her to support me for another four years of prolonged malfea-
sance. I had a shot at programs in Florida, Texas, Missouri, Ohio,
and Utah, and the Utah one looked particularly appealing. Pretty
much all we knew about Utah was that it had mountains and Mor-
mons, both austere and in good supply, and that my former teacher
and our dear friend Melanie Rae Thon lived there. She was as kind
and calming a person as she was sublime a short story writer and
novelist. She was my literary Joan of Arc. If anybody could help us,
it was she.

It felt wrong even to think about it, but it also felt grim and fa-
talistic to pass up the opportunity to get a PhD, which might lead

to an actual job and, I hoped, some long-term stability. My grandparents were thrilled at the prospect of having another doctor in the family, even if nobody would consider me a *real* doctor.

Thankfully, my mom's abdominal surgery went well, and the night she recovered in the hospital, I brought her a card my inmate students had signed, and I read *The Little Prince* to her, trying to calm and soothe us both. The mass was miraculously benign and no complications loomed, but it made everything feel fragile and my future plans all the more despicable.

I never thought I'd really get into any of the programs, but I did. And, well, we left for Utah.

We found a reasonably nice apartment in a part of Salt Lake City called The Avenues. School began for me, and Jenae got a job doing events for a swanky hotel, and things should have been looking up, but they weren't.

Gram's health got worse and worse as her present was lost to her past, and by the time spring came around, she couldn't tell us from her nurses' aides and almost all she knew for sure was her own childhood, de-tasseling corn and picking weeds in the bean fields. We lost more and more of her as she lost us, until finally she died, one month before Mother's Day.

A couple of weeks later, Bruce called, and it wasn't just to see how I was holding up. He and Emma had a few months ago given birth to a baby boy, and they were moving from Massachusetts back to Texas.

"What's up?" I asked. "You guys back in the big funky yet?"

I was driving back from school and took a detour through Federal Heights, just below the foothills. From Chandler Drive the entire Salt Lake Valley shimmered like a flammable mirage.

"Well, Matty boy," Bruce said, "I bet I got you trumped for bad news today." He exhaled smoke loudly into the phone. "Emma found out."

"Found out about what?" But as the words came out of my mouth, I knew. He'd been talking more and more over the past year about how batshit crazy everything was and how he didn't know if he could survive it for much longer. I knew he was miserable. What I didn't know was that he was, as he said then, "in pure-D love with another woman."

I felt deeply sorry and happy for him at the same time, but a little worried about what it might mean for Jenae and me. Bryan and Sarah, we would soon learn, were similarly heading toward divorce, and it was beginning to seem as if everything we once could count on was now made of lint.

"Bruce," I said. My compass had lost its points.

"Yeah," he said. "Shitfire."

Something needed to be done, and it wasn't going to do it by itself.

The way Jenae guided me through the darkness of my dad's and then Gram's death, I learned for good what I almost forgot: I *loved* my wife. It was time to really, not just ceremonially, do right by her.

So we decided to buy a house. I wanted her to have some outward sign of stability and thanks for all she'd done and endured over the years. But like getting married, deciding you are going to buy a house and actually buying a house are two very different endeavors.

Initially, things looked perfect. Interest rates were at an all-time low. The economy was in the gutter, and Alan Greenspan sent the APR down deep to buck things up. We did some quick computing and found that, at the best interest rates, we could own a nicer house than anyone we knew and pay less per month than we were currently paying in rent.

But between the banks' promises of immediate approval and the hours spent on hold listening to the Muzak version of "Don't Stop Believin'," something was wrong. Our credit was shit.

Mother's Day was fast approaching, and since Gram died my mom had been crying herself blind, working at her flower shop fourteen hours a day on arrangements for other people's mothers, so we decided to have Grandpa come out for the weekend. He had been strange and diffident with my mom, and she couldn't handle her grief, him, and the shop at the same time.

We thought we'd show Gramps the mountains, eat a steak or two, have a good cry, toast Gram with a glass of Dewar's (the only Scotch she'd drink), then pack him back on the plane after Mother's Day was over so we could all limp forward.

When he arrived, he was the last person off the plane. He didn't bother with a hug and started shuffling toward the exit. "Christ," he said, "do I need a drink."

It was only ten in the morning, so we drove up a foggy Emigration Canyon to Ruth's Diner and ordered bloody marys and waited for each other to say something inspiring.

Being with my grandfather is a bit like spending time with a retired colonel who had managed to escape great loss and infamy, as well as fame and recognition, during his years of service. And now that he's retired there is nothing left to do but soak up the impending sense of time left and great deeds undone. He had been a radiologist and a professor of medicine, and though I'm sure he has a passel of former patients and students who remain obliged to him, they aren't exactly hustling to finish up his bust for the Mayo Clinic.

To those who are not his grandson, my grandfather makes people nervous. He seems exacting and draconian. When he orders his drink, Gin-on-the-rocks-with-an-olive, all as one word, and you repeat it just to double-check, he barks back, *Gin-on-the-rocks-with-an-olive!* Mad, fast, and annoyed. He is a man who expects you to be incapable, ingratiating, and, in general, hungry for his money. You may bobble in your simpering, for example, and say, Yes sir, Mr. Tucker, but all he'll have heard was the grave omission of "Dr.," and you shall never be forgiven. After his cocktail, he is temporarily a changed man. He will want to know your name and where you are from and what your golf handicap is and what you think of black golfers and oversize drivers. But he'll tire of your response before you can stammer out the first phoneme of your name. If I were you, I'd give the table away the next time he comes in. He's a crappy tipper too.

When it's just Grandpa and me, however, things are different. Sometimes I get the sense that I am the one man in the world he feels he can talk to. Everyone else works for him or wants to or is afraid to. Me, I'm just a screw-up English major who can't keep himself straight without his help. I am his only grandson, after all, and more or less the son he always wanted. I've inherited his wavy hair. His preference for manual-transmission cars. His skeptic's furrowed brow. His way of radiating disapproval and judgment without word or gesture. His predilection for good, honest books and his general disdain for ones that tend to garner all the conspicuous prizes. His sadistic joy in teaching. His aversion to bullshit. His inherent, endemic loneliness.

When our similarities grow too obvious, we revert back to our archetypal roles of patriarch and prodigal son. Ostensibly, whatever we are talking about is a test. The question might be, How's your class going? Your short game doing any better? or How's the car running? But the real underlying question is always, You still can't take care of yourself, can you, Matt? You still have that weak follow-through, don't you? Still just a profligate little punk, aren't you? How much do you need? Just tell me. Give me a number.

There was a lot we weren't talking about.

Throughout Gram's descent into Alzheimer's, Grandpa was characteristically stoic. He never cried or showed any remorse or weakness — nothing really except a mild irritation at the brutish inevitability that comes with such a disease. To an outsider it would have looked cruel, but doubtless he would have acted the same if the illness were his own. As a physician, he was foremost a scientist whose job was to locate weakness and eliminate it, or acquiesce. With Alzheimer's the whole brain is the weakness, and that is pretty much that.

Beyond stern dismay, there was one moment, only a few seconds after Gram exhaled her last breath, when Grandpa kneeled at her side. He took both her hands in his and bowed his head and touched his cheek with her fingertips. "I'm sorry," he said. "Christ, Jean, I'm so sorry."

I thought he was apologizing for his distance and his insensitivity, or maybe for her long suffering through the disease and the arthritis, but my mom shook her head at Grandpa and took Gram's hands away from him. There seemed to be something my mom didn't want my grandmother to give him, even in death.

The next day, my mom and I drove to the Larsen Brothers Funeral Home, just up National Avenue from her flower shop. "Now that Gram can't be hurt anymore," she began, "you might as well know."

I was driving her Korean SUV and couldn't get the seat far enough back.

"Does this thing even work?" I said, jerking on the lever. "Know about what?"

Mom was holding Gram's heart-shaped gold locket in her hands like a rosary.

"Well," Mom said, "the one I expect will be the biggest trouble is named Ruth."

I pulled into the funeral home's parking lot, which it shared with Hardware Hank next door. "What do you mean, the one? What trouble?"

My entire life I had seen my grandfather as a reticent, stern work- and golf-aholic who knew the difference between having nothing and something to say. Suddenly it appeared that he had wanted to be somewhere he wasn't, with people who weren't us.

"Women," my mom said. "Trouble with women."

He drained his first bloody mary before the waiter had a chance to leave. He twirled his finger in the air to order another round. Not a popular gesture in Utah.

"So," he said, "what's this about wanting to buy a house? Your mother said you guys were thinking pretty seriously about it. How are your finances?"

I was not sure where he was headed, but if it was where I thought, I was sure I didn't want him buying a house for us.

"This thing got any hooch in it?" he said. He tilted his glass back and tried to shake more vodka from the ice. Our food had arrived but our second drink had not.

"It's Utah," I said. "Can't serve any drink with more than one ounce of alcohol in it." I had to explain the blue laws several times a day at the restaurant. It was not a topic I enjoyed, in conversation or in fact.

"One *ounce?*" he said. "That's barely enough to get the glass wet. No wonder you're so quiet."

I moved the gummy eggs around my plate and began to tell him euphemistically about our finances, but before I could finish he pushed himself back from the table and loosened his belt.

"I've been thinking," he said. He dropped his napkin on the rest of his eggs and shoved the plate out of his way, toward me, which nearly sent my plate into my lap.

"You're having a hard time with this loan, I gather," he said. He brushed a bit of egg from the lapel of his leather blazer.

"Yeah," I said.

Because he was bringing up the subject, it would be his idea to help, and that meant I wouldn't have anything to feel bad about. My mom and my grandma had told me all my life this one simple truth: it has to be his idea. You can have anything you want as long as he thinks it's his idea.

"There's all this talk of the low rates," I said, trying to sound savvy and calm. "And it's supposed to be such a buyer's market, but if people like me and Jenae can't get a loan, then who can?"

"That's right," he said, not like a cheer but a confirmation of a small bit of logic. He likes it when I try to talk business. He knows I'm not good at it. It's something he can count on. "The banks sure do like to give money to people who don't need it, like me," he said. "Which has got me thinking."

He tugged at the waistband of his corduroys.

He seemed excited about what he was going to say. It was probably the only thing he could be sure Gram would have wanted him to do and the only meaningful way he could salve whatever guilt or remorse he felt.

"Why don't I get the loan for you?"

It wasn't what I thought he was going to say. It was better. Less pathetic than his buying the thing outright; far more desirable than anything we'd be able to do on our own. And we'd be indebted to him for his credit, for a change, and not just his money.

"I'll talk to my accountant," he said, his favorite phrase in the English language. "Miss Ricketts is back in Peoria, so it might take a day or two. Meanwhile, I've gotta hit the little radiologists' room."

Chuck Norris Time

* * *

WITH GRANDPA ON BOARD, things were looking up, but thus far in our house-hunting endeavors we had succeeded at nothing. We still had no loan and no home picked out for sure. We had nothing but the shaky promise of my grandfather and the tacit employ of a pseudo-realtor — Sully. Realtor by day, waiter with me at The New Yorker by night, standup Mormon comedian in suburban, nonalcoholic strip-mall nightclubs on the weekends. You know, the usual.

Sully had shown us a ton of houses, but we hated every single one. We said we preferred older houses close to downtown; he showed us mock Tudors in developments adjacent to smorgasbord restaurants. We wanted something with hardwood floors and old double-hung windows; he showed us planned communities with streets named after obscure but famously violent Latter-Day Saints.

A native of Virginia and a father of three, Saul, or Sully as he likes to be called, is a six-foot-three Teutonic blond who would look as convincing in drag as he would in an SS uniform. It's a little odd, I suppose, for a licensed realtor to be a waiter as well, but until recently, when his wife opened a fancy shoe boutique in downtown Sugarhouse, he struggled to support his family on his lottery-like realty salary.

On any given excursion with Sully, whether it's to the stockroom to get more linens for a banquet of pharmaceutical reps or to the Marmalade Hill area in his thirdhand, perfunctory white Lexus to check out a promising new listing, we cover all the bases. One moment we'll be talking APRs and Greenspan's motivation and the fickle relativity of the tax base, the next we'll be running odds on whether our manager's back on cocaine and anonymous men's room sex, and then we'll debate the logic of one-firearm-per-daughter investing, the sad state of surfing in Utah, hamster rights, and everything on down that line — all in accents ranging from Gandhi to William Wallace to Hank Hill to Michael Jackson. To know Sully is to love Sully is to hate Sully. He's pleasantly schizophrenic, and talking to him is like trying to catch a Super Ball in a hall of mirrors.

Before we went with Sully, we thought that realtors could be people too, and had been working with one who was a graduate of the program I was in at school. Her name was Fiona, and she divided her time among realty, skiing, and writing.

"Shop around, you know," she said. "Take it easy, see what feels right, you know. Give me a call when you want to get together on something."

Cool, we thought.

We had been house shopping for only a couple of weeks when we found one we liked more than we imagined possible. Everything was right about it. Good street, good street name: Denver. The incidental city of my birth. Last name of modern-day bard and world-champion drinker-and-driver John Denver. The address was a palindrome. It was near a junk store, a coffee shop, a ta-queria, a Vietnamese grocery/nail salon/jewelry store, and a great big park. Close enough to green space to keep the spaniel happy, close enough to downtown to keep our street cred.

That Sunday we hurried through an open house and found it nice enough. It needed some paint, the floors were a little scuffed, and it backed up to some kind of medical surplus warehouse, but what the hell. It was The House, we decided. We hadn't made any official arrangement with Fiona and didn't actually have her number, so it was by chance that we ran into her at a party that night.

"Guess what!" we said. "We found the one!" We were going to blow our lifetime allotment of exclamation marks on this deal, we knew, but it was going to be worth it!

We told her where it was and what it was like as she nodded. She began to move from mellow attention to a kind of bemused concern. She said she thought she knew the house we were talking about. She'd give us a holler soon and we'd figure things out.

The next day, she called with what she described as "funny news."

"As it turns out," Fiona said, "I *had* seen that house on Denver." She paused here, trying to figure out how funny the next bit would be to us. "A couple who's in the program with you at the U actually just had me write up an offer on it."

Realtors are apparently exempted from the normal space-time continuum. Time, as they experience it, is at once slower and faster — the way the world spins at over a thousand miles an hour but looks still and placid from far enough away. They understand in ways that most buyers and sellers never will that a house for sale is a trifling thing. As monumental as tuna salad, say, if not for all the paperwork.

We *liked* Fiona. We liked the couple in question. We all were

English-major types at the university, and there weren't many to spare on that side of the Rockies. But it would be a while before we would be liking any of them in an active, let's-go-for-twist-cones! kind of way.

We needed to start over.

In realty, some agents are the typical coffee-addled, business-card-palming, bright-pennies-in-their-loafers folks. A few are more like anti-agents. Unrealtors. Dealing with them is like trying to get a lifelong beach bum to embrace the subtle but sexless joys of patent law or philately. Their appeal, apparently, is that they are so not going to pressure you into anything. In fact, they are not so much your realtor as they are your bud.

Sully and I had been buddies at work from the day we met. But our relationship took a significant turn the day I said, "Oh, hey, you're a realtor, right?"

Cue eyebrow. Dramatic pause.

It was a stupid question, because his business cards were every-where in the restaurant. Taped to the employee lockers in the break room. Stuck on the hostess's stand next to prominent reservations. Hanging from the wait station's air conditioning ducts. The card was oriented vertically, and three-quarters of it was taken up with a head shot of Sully doing his Hey!-I'm-Sully-and-you-are? smile, but until he physically gave me one, I thought they were tickets for one of his standup gigs.

When I asked Sully the obvious question, he didn't so much con-sider it as he did morph from Waiter Sully to — *shazam!* — Real-tor Sully. "Why jes, capitán," he said. "Yo soy realtor. Y tu mamá?"

Sully and I were polishing racks of wine glasses. It was nearly midnight, and I thought we were just making idle banter to get through the rest of the shift. Eight hours later, however, Sully picked me up in his Lexus and chauffeured me around to a dozen or so houses, and we made plans to do the same thing the next day. Having Sully for an agent was like being courted by Superman while he's between archenemies, so he's devoted his powers to helping you with more enthusiasm than you really desired.

Practically every day would be an opportunity for his domestic heroism. It wasn't something you could predict or force; it was spontaneous. You'd be sitting around surfing the Internet for new listings and better interest rates when, out of the blue, your phone would ring. It's Sully calling from the office, and you can tell he's very busy because phones and faxes and alarms are ringing in the background and he's yes-ing and no-ing some assistant. But he's paying attention, really he is, and he was just wondering what you were doing for lunch, because if you didn't have any plans, sugar (a Deep South, sweet-tea, slow-fan accent), he'd luuuv to take you for a quick bite and then check out (in his Tom Brokaw Great Plains anchor voice) a promising investment opportunity he found this morning, but it's "a wee bet south" — and we're in Scotland now, his voice draped in plaid — "though Eee know it's farrrtharrr doun than yee want, 'tis a far bet cheepper, what d'ye say, laddee?"

He was hard to resist, unless you were actually Scottish, say, or a Southerner. Otherwise, he has a way of making you feel, well, special. Sully knows that buying a house is about as emotional and traumatic and exciting an endeavor a couple can undertake, just short of getting married and having kids. Sure, some folks would have us believe that buying a house is not that different from buying a used car or a bicycle or a box of donuts. For the rest of us — the ambulatory ones with the ability to fog mirrors — buying a house is the most daunting thing imaginable. Having a kid, well, we're talking about a freaking miracle, not something that any mortal can truly take full responsibility for. Sure, there are the right schools and college funds and that fine art of knowing when to stop or start the corporal punishment, but the procurement of a kid is the result of—what?—fifteen to twenty seconds of, shall we say, impulsiveness. Getting married is kind of the same. Again, it's practically a miracle if you can actually find somebody who will not only share a meal with you, but a bed and, my God, a bathroom too. A house, on the other hand, that's nothing to be impulsive about. Houses are heavy, for one thing. And worse, they don't say much. Not at first. Not about who they really are. There's hardly any getting to know a house until you're fully committed, blindfolded and swan-diving into what might be a very dry pool.

When looking for a house, you're not looking for mere lumber and plumbing but rather for spirit and community. You're not looking for a location but a locus, a place that will be your center. A place from which you'll leave every day, only to return, just before dark, brown bags of sustenance in your arms. The house we pick is the most stationary and permanent fixture of our lives, and it's not only how others will see us in relation to it, but how we see ourselves. The house where you live literally dictates where you will sleep, where you will walk, where you will eat, where you will love, laugh, and perhaps procreate. The kind of light you see, the hearth you'll tend, the water you will drink.

Sully, despite his Saturday-morning cartoon antics, knew. Sully also knew that providence plays a lesser role than persistence when it comes to finding The House. Because what The House is, of course, is a decision, an approximation, a negotiation, a concession even.

He tried to tell us, tried to coach us in his best Mr. Miyagi spirit. "Matthew-san, Jenae-san must focus powah." He jerked his tie from his neck and ceremonially cinched it around my head. "No think in Batt time. Think in house time. Batt time short. House time like karate time. You know, Chuck Norris time. House time long time."

It was June now, and we were getting a bit tense about the whole process. We were still waiting for our banker in Peoria, Miss Ricketts, to get our financing together. My grandfather kept telling me he trusted us and that we should go ahead and pick a place. We wanted to be in a house by the time our lease was up on August 1, but it was beginning to look bleak.

Early one Tuesday morning, as I waited for Sully to pick me up so we could check out some prospects closer to downtown before we both had to be at work, I was nosing around on a realty website and saw something unusual. There was no picture, but the description of the house, the location, square footage, street name — everything started gaining momentum, and when Sully showed up I said, "I think we need to see this."

Whenever I'd show him a listing, he'd take a quick, dismissive glance, the way you might take in a dentist's shoes, and then hand back whatever sheet I gave him and proceed to regale me with how many years that house had been on the market, how many different agents had listed it, and how many times they'd repainted the front door, trying to fool the market into thinking it was a new house. I could tell that Sully was a little hurt by my perusing the Internet, looking at the public Multiple Listing Service hoping to find something his professional, supercharged search engine couldn't. But the fact is that realtors get new listings only once a week. Chances are, in a good, vibrant market, if a house is priced fairly and in decent shape, it'll move. If it's overpriced or shoddily kept up, it'll rot. So I cruised the websites.

Sully saw right away that what I'd found wasn't an old listing. It had a new MLS number, and in his years as a realtor he'd never seen it. He knew the street and he knew what kind of money a house on it could pull, and this one was asking about ten grand below that. That probably meant it "Needs Some TLC" (knotty pine) or it is a "Great Starter Home" (really freaking small, so you'd better love each other) or it is "Gorgeous on the Inside" (crack vial mosaics on the steps, nine-millimeter shell-casing wind chimes).

We pulled onto the street to find a quiet, tree-lined affair between a busy eight-lane artery at the far end and a calm, walkin'-my-baby-back-home avenue at the other. A little dissonance could be good, I thought. We cruised the street looking for the telltale realtor's yardarm. There was none. Sully called the listing agent and briefly did his shop talk (I know! Wants you to drop to five percent? Why not throw in your youngest daughter. Am I right?) while I stared at the house across the street.

It wasn't the kind of *Gone with the Wind* deal where the place is so grand you give it a name, as though it were your offspring, but still, it was something. Solid. Nice. White-painted brick with a little driveway and a garage in back. Out front was a huge pine tree, big enough to shade the whole house, including a great wooden porch that was just high enough to let you feel superior to street-level people but not ostentatiously so. Double-hung windows framed the front door on either side, and overall the house looked smallish but well balanced for its square footage compared to a lot of others we'd seen. It was the difference between dressing an adult in a well-tailored suit and shoehorning a fat grownup into a child's clothes.

"Thar she blows, skipper," Sully said, but like a drag queen instead of Ahab. "Wanna have a peep?"

He did this talk-show-host, fake tie-straightening thing with the air in front of his silky yellow golf shirt, and in a half-Telemundo, half–Peter Lorre voice he said, "Jou is nehver going to a belief dis, boss. Éste house, jou know? It only arrive on dee market here dis mornin. We here is dee first peoples to have see it."

With that, he winked and rang the doorbell.

"This is all very good," he said in his realtor-friend voice. He patted me on the shoulder and we waited for the door to open.

Inside, there was a mommy with a newbie in her arms and a full-size American poodle bounding up and down and all around as though we were made of kibble. The smell of apple cobbler wafted out and made me think of my grandma's from-scratch cinnamon rolls.

It was an old trick, but even Sully had to admit, a nice touch. The lady put her kid in a jogging stroller, harnessed the poodle, and told us to make ourselves at home. She seemed equal parts weepy, giddy, and needy. I can only imagine all the competing emotions and hormones, what with having a baby, getting ready to move, and selling a house. Short of starting a new job on top of it all, could it get more stressful?

Patsy Cline was on the stereo, and as I looked around the cozy, crayon-yellow living room, with its everything-old-is-new-again shag carpeting and overstuffed furniture, the hardwood-floored kitchen, the small but embraceable bedroom and beyond, I thought, I'm here. I'm *home.*

I called Jenae and told her to drop everything. "Get your maracas over here as soon as possible," I said.

"Excuse me?" she said. Sully was clearly wearing off on me, and it wasn't always thrilling for Jenae or anybody else within earshot.

While I poked around, Sully called the selling agent and tried to hype her up and get her ready for an offer. From what I could tell, these folks could easily be the five-years-older version of Jenae and me. They had funky black-and-white photos on the wall — including some semi-nude pregnancy pics I wouldn't have displayed, never mind how artistic, but still — and lots of chunky, thrift store furniture that spoke as much of savings as it did world view. One small bedroom looked to be a kind of writing office and music studio, replete with a Gibson Les Paul leaning against a Fender Bluesman, an Underwood typewriter hulking like a godfather next to a new Mac laptop. The other little bedroom was a baby room, done in politically savvy, gender-neutral sea-foam greens and pale yellows. The kitchen was a tight but well-designed galley with nice knives, a professional mixer, and a gas stove. The basement featured a small workout space with a yoga mat and weights, and I noticed they had a bunch of backpacking and rock-climbing equipment. Outside, they had a fastidiously kept garden, fully mulched, a great little redwood deck with a pergola, and two cute suspended hammock chairs, perfect for curling up on a summer's eve to read poesy each to each.

Sully was just getting off the phone when a couple of semi-young folks came up the driveway, trailed by a man wearing a blond blazer that matched his mustache and pompadour. A good person would have told them to just hop on in and that the owner was out for a walk. A bad person would have grabbed Sully around the waist and said something like, "Sorry, there's been a mistake. My partner and I have decided not to sell. Good luck." We just gave them the stink-eye and waited.

Jenae showed up, did a thirty-second tour, and said, "All right." It had only been a week since we broke up with Fiona and lost that first house. When we told Sully it was a go, it felt like a rebound sort of move, a hopeless grab at something beyond our reach, and a test of our new relationship with Sully. He knew we were still waiting on some of the financing to go through and that we were a few weeks away from any kind of actual money, but he told us the place was ours.

"How can you be so sure?" I asked. I reminded him that we'd been burned by another house three blocks away from this one.

"Simple," Sully said. He licked his thumb and smoothed the pleats on his khakis. Then he licked again and touched the newel post. "Dibs," he said.

I had to work that night, so the plan was to have Jenae and Sully get everything ready while I was at the restaurant. Then, as soon as I got off, I'd go to his office, sign by all the little X's, and we'd fax over the offer. It'd all be wrapped up by first light.

I ended up having to stay until closing time, so when I called at eleven, I thought Jenae and Sully would be playing Boggle they'd be so bored. As it turned out, they were still hard at work. While I had been dropping dishes and swearing at known violent offenders and illegal foreign nationals at the restaurant, they had heard from the seller's realtor. By six P.M. she had received three offers, not including ours. So instead of playing nice, the sellers wanted a statement of preapproval for a loan, a written offer, and, unbelievably, a personal letter.

We were at Sully's office until nearly two A.M. By the time we were done, choruses of angels and orchestras of virgins were singing timeless arias about what beautiful people like us could do with a little patience, faith, coconut mulch, and latex paint.

No matter how many verses we could get out of our castrati, however, my grandpa couldn't get in touch with Miss Ricketts in the depths of her Peoria midnight.

Sully was relentless with his whole-lotta-love routine. He was sure they'd take our offer, if not adopt us. Preapproval to him meant next to nothing. "After all," he said, "we're not trying to close on the house tomorrow. Preapproval schmreeapproval."

* * *

When we didn't hear anything before I went to work at ten-thirty A.M., I knew. They had accepted another offer and were busy making the pretty little coronation bouquets and nosegays and couldn't yet bother telling us that we had lost.

Business at the restaurant was slow, and my only table was a couple of yuppie pricks wearing golf shirts from a course whose greens fees were higher than a month of my rent. They sat sprawling expansively in their booth, as though to express their masculinity, literally, in real estate.

I was bitterly refilling their Arnold Palmers when Carole, the matron of the waitstaff, touched my elbow and told me I had a call. I took it in the coat check closet.

"Hey, buddy," Sully said. It could not be good news. He was talking like a human being.

It was neither Friend Sully nor Realtor Sully. It was Elder Saul. The Elder Saul that was presiding over the funeral of our dream.

He told me about how much the sellers loved our letter, how they struggled all morning making their decision. "But," he said, "another buyer put up forty large in cash."

"That's just fucking great," I said.

Elder Saul was silent. He didn't handle cursing well. I looked around for something to break. There were only coat hangers, buckets of anise mints, and Carole's face, which my profanity had drained entirely of blood.

"What you need is a cheap and easy comeback house," he said, ignoring my murderous mood. "I know this skanky duplex over in West Valley City. We could grab some chalupas and head over there for a little picnic after your shift. What you say, chica?"

I am a bad person. I was pissed off.

Sully was already way over it. For him, there hadn't even been an "it."

I think he knew that this was the time when realtors write their own checks. Now that our hearts had been broken, we'd be looking for something with a roof and a door or two, nothing particular, just get it over with. Gimme shelter. That's all.

"Or we could stay the course," he said, shifting gears. "There's this dapper little bungalow a hop, skip, and a dump away?"

I told him I didn't think so.

"Come on, Matthew-san," he tried. I'll give him that; he tried. His Miyagi voice made me remember his tie and that apple cobbler and then I was right back in the foyer of the house I'd never live in, the ghost of my grandmother baking away for other people's children. "Remember house time?" he said. "Chuck Norris?" he said. "Time?"

"Fuck Chuck," I said. "I got food dying in the window. I'll see you tomorrow."

"Okey-dokey," he said.

I felt like Oedipus, post–eye/fork incident. And yet right after I got back on the floor, my friend Susan asked if we got the house.

She is one of the five kindest people on this earth. She's worked with at-risk teenagers and has a dog named Ezekiel. She is a poet and has crazy curly hair like mine. I wanted to make her cry.

"No," I said. "Didn't work out."

"Oh, yippee!" she said. Her exclamation point felt like an ice pick. "Now's when you find the house you were really meant to have!"

"Great," I said. I didn't know what she meant, but I knew it was more positive than I could handle at the moment. "Zip-a-dee-fucking-doo-dah."

South of Bountiful

GRAM AND I WOULD stay up long into the small hours, drinking Dewar's and eating oyster crackers, talking about how the Hoosiers look like real contenders this year, about how overworked Mom was, about how big a jerkoff everyone named Bob was. Bob, my mom's newest, third husband. Bob, Gram's own husband. Bobby Knight, she said, got a bye. I thought we were mostly kidding. She was a dear heart of a woman, but she was also fiercely protective of the people she loved — pretty much just me and my mom. She always said, hoisting her Scotch high, "You are going to get what you deserve, damn it. I didn't stay with him for all these years for nothing!"

I thought she was hilarious.

I didn't really think about what she was saying then. If I did, I shrugged it off as her being a little harder than necessary on Grandpa's lack of conversational polish or on my mom's newest husband's uncouth Cudahy ways. I certainly never imagined that she spent her whole life married to a man she hated just so she could afford a better one for her daughter and her grandson.

The story, as I half remember, half imagine it — it was not a popular fairy tale growing up — starts with when she was a nursing student at Indiana University. She had caught tuberculosis and was quarantined in the TB ward where my grandfather, a med student, was doing his rotation. They hadn't met before. With most of her ward mates being as attractive as anyone with consumption can be, he must have been a welcome sight.

After her release, my grandfather persuaded her to spend time with him, since he had a colleague's old Hudson convertible at his disposal. It didn't hurt, of course, that he was going to be a doctor, and that he had a some land up in Shelby County near her hometown of Pendleton, Indiana. When he asked her to marry him, however, she said no.

"He was good-looking enough, I suppose," she said, "for the second son of a pig farmer."

Gram spun the ice in her glass and watched it whirl.

"That was almost fifty years ago, if you can believe that." She shook her head and held the empty glass. "Anyway, he asked for my hand." She looked at the dark picture window, now covered with fluttering moths, and turned her mouth somehow both down and into a smile. "'I don't believe I care to' is exactly what I said to that. I thought a very good deal of myself back then, as you might imagine."

She shook her head and looked into her glass.

"But soon enough, well, everybody was joining the Army to improve their chances of staying stateside instead of being drafted and sent Lord knows where. Married couples got better picks and better accommodations, if you could call them that. They weren't, it turned out. Smartest thing I ever did was to say no to that man. But I didn't say it enough, now, did I?"

She got up to close the shade on the picture window. "Not very nice of me to torment those poor moths," she said, dropping the blind. "What they think they're missing in here I'm sure I'll never know."

Now, in the weeks after Gram's death, something was wrong with my grandfather. He was not sleeping. He was losing weight. He was drinking more and more. And he was having a harder time urinating. "Probably that goddamned prostate," he said over the phone. "There never has been any cure for getting old."

It wasn't what we wanted, to lose both of them. But still, Mom and I felt an odd sense of relief. If Grandpa was really ill, surely the nonsense with his — former? current? — lover named Ruth would have to end. It was almost as if we could finally say, Thank God — now we know it can't get worse.

All our lives, my mother and I knew my grandfather through his obstinacy, his meaty silence. He was not an uncomplicated man. When he was called in to work or went out to fetch pralines and cream, my mom, my grandmother, and I spent much of the time trying to figure out what he was thinking, what he would say, what would make him talk.

It was not entirely unpleasant. His words were simple and direct, and interpretation was generally uncalled for. He said what he meant, leaving little cause for wonder. I have inherited his sometime stoniness, and hear him through my reticence.

That all changed after Gram died. Not with him and me: between us talk was business — good business — about school, about work, about books — but business nonetheless. Then, within days of Gram's death, bouts of loquaciousness came over him. His thoughts were as odd as they were suddenly frequent — both because they were what they were, and because they were at all.

One night, Grandpa, Bob, and I were waiting for my mom and

Jenae to meet us at the Grandview Inn in Waukesha for dinner. It was two days after the funeral, and Jenae and I would be leaving for Utah soon. It seemed like a good idea to get out of the house. My mom had to do the flowers for somebody else's funeral that afternoon, and Jenae went to help, so the three of us sat, woman-less, at the bar. We ate pretzels and watched a recap of the Masters. There was nothing to talk about except when were Mom and Jenae going to get there. My grandpa ordered a second gin on the rocks — never a good sign.

"Do you know," he said, staring up at the TV, "how long it's been since I had sex?"

I thought I may have confused something Dick Enberg said on the overhead TV. Bob did not show any signs of hearing — which was not unusual: he too was an elderly man, only a handful of years younger than my grandfather. I looked at Grandpa. He was watching the TV. I looked at the TV. Golf. Nothing but golf. Green fields and putters. I said nothing.

The words continued to wrap around the inside of my skull — *Do you know how long it's been since I had sex?* — as though a teenager were toilet-papering my head.

"No," I said softly.

He just shook his head.

Shortly thereafter, my mom and Jenae showed up and the maitre d' took us to a table with six chairs. My mom sobbed into a napkin while a busboy got rid of the extra chair.

"It's a sickness," my mom had said. "He's a sick man."

With Gram cremated, and me safely back in Salt Lake City, my mom began to tell me things. Some things that she had known. Some things that she was just discovering. Things that both of us could very well have gone without knowing.

It all started the night when Gram got suspicious enough to pack my mom, twelve years old at the time, into her Buick and drive her all around Pekin looking for his bottom-of-the-line Porsche in the driveways of various women. Pekin was and is a small, chatty city, one where secrets were as poorly kept as they were prolific. My mom couldn't get down low enough in the passenger seat.

Now, she told me, there are at least three women.

Ruth was sixty-something. She was a radiology tech back in Pekin. She lives with her daughter in Indianapolis, and while no one knows how long it had been since they'd seen each other, as soon as Gram died, Grandpa started talking to her and flying out to see her. They've been having an on-again, off-again affair for decades. Ten years longer, in fact, than I have been alive.

Lorraine was in her seventies. Quite soon after Gram died, my mom decided Grandpa needed some age-appropriate company and tried to set him up with a few of her elderly neighbors and customers. Better than Ruth, she thought, who was about the same age as my mom. My grandfather went out with five or six ladies within a couple of weeks but found all of them, except Lorraine, boring and self-absorbed. "All they want to talk about is their goddamned angina," he said. "You're old," he told them. "What do you want me to do about it?"

And then there was Tonya.

Tonya was a nurse's aide who helped take care of Gram three days a week. This was in the last few months, when a squad of helpers settled into the condo. Nurses, nurses' aides, social workers — they were all good women, all with empathetic eyes and pursed lips, but they turned my grandparents' home into a kind of field hospital, and as much as we wanted them gone, their final absence would mean only one terrible thing.

Tonya smelled like a bowling alley and had a swagger that was at

once undermined and exaggerated by her scrubs, which had but-
terflies on them. The other nurses' aides stayed busy and moved
quickly, as if they might wreck the furniture if they lit upon it.
After Tonya got Gram into bed, she'd plop down on the couch or
on Gram's own chair, kick her feet up on the coffee table, and reach
for the bowl of nuts.

"Jesus," she'd say, "that's a lot of work."

Tonya came to the funeral with her ex-husband/now-boyfriend.
She wore a yellow dress fit for an Easter pageant, and the two of
them gamboled through the narthex as though they were selling
Fort Lauderdale time-shares. A week after the funeral, she started
coming around again, at three in the afternoon, just like she used
to, on Mondays, Wednesdays, and Fridays.

"She says she's worried about me," my grandfather explained.
"It's just for a little while."

"She's a goldbagger," my mom said to me. "A golddigger — whatever. I don't like it one bit."

It was May, and Gram had been gone a month, and I admitted
to my mother that I didn't like it either. "But he's *Grandpa,*" I said,
as if a de facto statement of his relation to me would at once describe and prescribe, render him back to the quiet elderly man who
always had batteries for my toys, who laughed out loud at Victor
Borge, a man for whom a foxtrot is damned near reckless.

I was supposed to be the smart one in the family. My mom
wanted to know now what everything meant. And because you
can only say "I don't know" for so long, I did what I have done
most of my life: made shit up.

"We're all dealing with loss in our own ways, Mom," I said. My
voice was draped in tweedy condescension. I was a teacher, a doctoral candidate; I knew what I was talking about. I was *smart.*

But that was bullshit. There are times when communication should be illegal, subjects absolutely forbidden. This was certainly one of them, and I'm using it here as a dramatic expository backdrop for my own life story. I didn't know what to do then, and I don't know what to do now, but we need to believe in something — if not our actual lives as they are lived, then at least the stories we can distill from them.

But to my mom I talked about pain the way Kant talked about music, which is to say, briefly and without regard to the fact that it has its own life, its own categorical imperatives.

"Think about it, Mom," I said. "He's displacing all the energy and time and life he had put into caring for Gram into something new, something that makes him feel necessary again. It's a terrible thing," I told her, "to feel useless."

It is true, what I said. It is false.

"I know, Matt," she said. "Jesus Christ, do I know."

My mom kept setting Grandpa up with her golf-league widows, and one by one my grandfather dismissed them to their knitting. All the while he was flying back and forth between Milwaukee and Indianapolis to see Ruth. Tonya was "stopping by" who knows when or how often, except that the crystal ashtray on his coffee table, usually filled with peanut M&M's, was lately choked with cigarette butts, and the recycling bin in his garage was overflowing with cans of domestic beer he never drank.

Meanwhile, his doctor expressed some concern over Grandpa's prostate, and he had been scheduled to undergo radiation therapy in lieu of surgery. I was useless in Salt Lake, but my mom was confident it would turn out to be a good thing.

"I know it's terrible," she told me, "but I think it's what we need. It'll knock some sense into him. And he won't be able to take care of himself, so I will, and I promised Gram — she made me *swear* — that I wouldn't put him in a home. I said I'm going to take care of him," she said, "and that's what I'm going to do."

One day in June, I found myself talking to my grandpa on my cell phone. I was driving on 11th Avenue, well above the Salt Lake Valley floor, and that day it smelled of sulfur and smoke and the air was a hazy yellow-brown from a wildfire north of Bountiful, where I taught a class. Heretofore in my life, wildfires were what happened in wildest Montana or in the thankless San Bernardino Mountains. They were wilderness fires. They weren't supposed to sneak up on you while you were commuting to work.

"Well, I guess you should know," Grandpa said without preface or segue. "The big news here is that Tonya and I are pretty serious."

This was six, maybe seven weeks after Gram died.

It was over a hundred degrees. My truck was already near overheating, the air was the color of punishment, and my grandfather was telling me something about a woman who eats cigarettes and shoe leather.

"What does that mean?" I asked. "'Serious.'" There was a stop sign. It made sense. I knew what I was supposed to do.

"Well," my grandpa said, terse and cornered. "I guess it means that we care an awful lot about each other, Matt."

"Okay," I said. "I don't know that I understand."

I had always fancied myself a pretty empathetic guy. A writer. A waiter. A teacher. Someone who knew how to listen and let people know that I was listening without being ostentatious about it. At this moment, the sonic experience of my listening must have sounded like a needle bouncing and scratching near the spinning center of a record.

"You know, Matt," my grandfather said. It was his own teacher's voice. The voice that had told me such things as *Take the club back as far as you can, and then take it back another foot.* "What all men really want," he said, "is a trophy wife. I guess you know that."

I don't remember the end of that conversation. I don't remember how I arrived at school. I don't remember how I taught grammar, syntax, and style for an hour and a half.

I do remember having to stop several times on my commute to add coolant to my overheating, ancient Land Cruiser. And I do remember the fire. At least I think I remember the fire. Something was on fire that whole summer. I remember the smoke. I remember the swirling, sepia skies. I remember those hopelessly little planes swooping down, dumping tiny buckets of water on a fire the size of a mountain.

On Moving On

ON OUR STREET in The Avenues, kids ride garbage cans down the mile-long hill, steep as a luge run. They're tall, barrel-shaped cans with two wheels on the bottom and an attached lid on top, and the kids jump inside them as though into a sleeping bag, aim feet-first downhill, and torpedo out of sight. From 11th Avenue to 3rd, there are no controlled intersections on our street, so whether you're in a garbage can or on a skateboard or any other wheeled vehicle, you'll be doing sixty by the time you hit the first stop sign.

In the nine or so months that we've lived there, I have called 911 for accidents three times from my porch. Also, the people who lived in our apartment before us (they bought a house a couple of blocks away in hopes of rejuvenating their marriage) are getting divorced. And their dog, Kilo (yes, as in kilogram — the husband smoked a lot of dope), recently got hit by a car. The guy's dog in the apartment next to ours also got hit by a car. The guy was an artist, already divorced, and his current girlfriend is clinically insane and has poured mineral spirits on one of his paintings and threatened to burn the whole place down. Jenae is convinced our apartment is haunted. I don't argue. Ghost or no ghost, there's certainly a disturbance and things are getting worse and it isn't just our apartment.

Somebody with a BB gun went through the neighborhood and shot out fifty-six car windows, including two of Jenae's. Then people started finding dead cats all over the neighborhood, their disemboweled corpses draped around the shrubbery like so much gory tinsel. Some said it was a case of satanic ritual killing. Others said it wouldn't have been the first cougar to come down to the valley. And nobody knew what had become of Elizabeth Smart, the fifteen-year-old girl kidnapped from her bedroom a few blocks away, until they found her wandering around the city in a burka, quietly pleading for help behind her veil.

It is time to skedaddle.

Stanley's house is far from perfect. It's almost a hundred years old and looks it in most ways. The structure seems fine, but it's going to take more than a little willpower and sandpaper to put it right. The furnace has to go, as do all the appliances, and it has more wood paneling and shag carpeting than the set of *The Partridge Family* and smells as if generations of actual fowl have lived there.

The night after I saw the house and met Stanley, I drive past the refineries, strip clubs, and quarries to teach, thinking that there is no way Jenae will go for it, but she agrees to check it out.

She goes with Sully to see the house while I am in class. It seems ridiculous to have her go without me along, but Stanley did say that that Oriental girl was about ready to put in an offer, and given our recent luck, if we don't act fast, we might as well give up. In every way, this feels like our last chance.

I am not optimistic. I think I'll get home from teaching and she'll slap me for suggesting that we live in such a dump. Then I will quietly concede and we'll simply stay put and get killed on I Street by a kid inside a garbage can, mauled by mountain lions, or abducted by psychotic fundamentalists.

When I do get back from teaching, we sit on the front porch of our apartment watching traffic fly by, cocktails between us, and talk about the house. It's nearly nine o'clock, and it is still so hot that the sweat on our faces gleams in the last light of day. Our dog Maggie is lying on her back in the burnt grass, her legs straight up in the air.

"Was Stanley still wearing his shorts?" I ask.

Jenae takes a sip of her drink. "I don't want to talk about it," she says. "His shorts."

"What did Sully say?"

"You know," she says.

She has our fat orange and white cat, Skillet, hooked up to his small-dog harness. We named him that because, when we first got him, he liked to sleep in a frying pan. Now he's panting as though he were in a hot one. It's really unattractive.

"He was doing his Indian 'And vhat do you tink?' thing," she says. A car zooms by as if it has been dropped from a plane. Jenae scoops Skillet into her lap and closes her eyes.

"Did he do his reach test?" I ask. This is when Sully stands next to a wall and tries to touch the ceiling, his reach having been measured at an impressive ten feet.

"Yes," Jenae says. She smiles. "Over nine feet."

"Well then."

Jenae sips her drink and coughs a little. I wasn't pouring short that night. She looks at me and takes another sip. I ask her if Stanley said anything about other prospective buyers.

"Like 'Orientals' with tape measures?" she says.

"She makes me nervous," I say.

"Bigot."

We smile without looking at each other.

It's getting dark, but a thin crown of light remains, making the Salt Lake Valley feel like a dim, golden bowl. A pair of kids on bikes zip past. I hear them before I can see them, and then they are gone. Jenae and I hold our breath and wait for the crash, but it doesn't come.

"Let's get the hell out of here," she says. "Three's a charm, right?"

"Right-o," I say. "Let's do it."

Despite all the sadness and pain of the past three months, the oddities of real estate, the throes of getting a loan secured via the mysterious Miss Ricketts via my philandering grandpa via my dead beatific grandmother — despite all the houses we've loved and lost, even this one, which may well get snatched up by a tape-measure-wielding foreigner — it hasn't been a bad way to spend a summer. Looking for a house as we've done, instead of just staying put or buying whatever we could afford, in whatever imitation suburb of whatever imitation city, not giving in, not giving up, but struggling and searching and scouring and driving and walking and biking and hiking around every damned last nook, cranny, corner, and brook of our chosen city, we found our new favorite place — sweet, sweet Sugarhouse, named for the bounty of sugarbeets it used to produce. And who knows? Maybe we've found ourselves at home there.

We are getting good at this by now. We write up the offer in minutes and Sully faxes it to Stanley and overnight we wait. I don't really believe Stanley has a fax machine. I expect it to take days to hear from him because I imagine he gave us the fax number for the small-arms supplier his militia uses, but the next day when I get back from my lunch shift, there's already a message from Sully.

"Hey guys, hey Jenae, hey Matt. Und hello little Skeeleet and Maagae. Listen, Matt, I've got this improv thing down in Sandy tomorrow and thought you might want to pick up my shift." I stand in front of our answering machine, afraid to take off my waiter's clothes. Maggie sniffs vigorously at the scents of the restaurant as Sully's message continues. "But, you know, if you don't want to do it, Carole's such a shift whore I'm sure she'll take it or farm it out to one of her minions, and oh voy! I got the paperwork back from Stanley and it all looks like we're ready to roll, Mr. and Mrs. Jefferson. We're movin' on up to the east side. So I'll get back to it here, and you can let me know about that shift — by tonight would be great. Peas and carrots. Sully out."

I call Jenae and ceremoniously tell her I have news.

"Yeah?" she says.

"Yup," I say.

"So that's it?" she says.

I say I guess so. Neither of us really believes it's true.

She gets a bottle of champagne to celebrate with, but I have to work a double, and by the time I get home from the restaurant she's asleep on the couch.

It was the most exciting night of our lives. We were exhausted.

In most ways, buying a new bike, adopting a kitten, getting your braces taken off, or even lancing a boil is more dramatic than the actual purchase of a house. With just about anything else there is at least a palpable before and after. But with a house it's more like: Well, here's the house without me standing in front of it and — next slide — here's me standing in front of the house. After all, unless you do something fairly seismic, the house and the land it's on will be bought and sold long after you have left your paw prints all over the place.

After working a meager lunch shift I scoot over to the house, because Sully had said Stanley had some new hollow-core doors he got on sale at a surplus store that he was going to throw in for free.

I catch Stanley in the act of putting one up and try to make my case without sounding unappreciative. "You know," I say, "there's something about these old doors."

Stanley looks at me and twitches his mustache. "Yeah?" he says.

"Yeah," I say. "They've got — I don't know — character."

"Character," I realize as it comes out of my mouth, is about as generic a term as possible for something you like but cannot name and/or afford in real estate. When I went on a postgraduation tour of Europe with my friend Flavio, I noticed we kept falling back on the term "architecture" to describe what we liked about the churches and museums. But as an adjective, "architecture," like "character," means something you think is ineffable is really just beyond your vocabulary.

Stanley looks at the old doors and scratches his butt. "Well," he says, "they're old." He points with his thumb at the new doors. They look as if they were made of peanut brittle, then scratched by a cat to get that faux wood-grain texture. "I got these new ones here ready to go. They're real nice. Light. Easy to close. Easy to open."

"What can I say?" I say. "The wife likes 'em." That such a phrase could even issue from my head shocks me. I am not a guy who blames his wife for things. I am beginning to realize, however, that this is an all-access, no-explanation-needed pass to do that which is regrettable, especially in front of other men.

"*Wimin,*" Stanley says, pursing his lips and shaking his head, as if he'd almost managed to forget about them.

The truth is I want those old doors as much as she does. I remember being a kid and living in a very prefabricated, postwar, disposable apartment building where everything was foam-core or hollow. I'd try to throw a respectable tantrum and storm off to my room and slam the door, only to have it whiff shut. I soon found I could punch through the walls even though I barely outweighed a telephone book.

Stanley and I talk about the projects he's been working on and what he'd do, if he were me, to keep the place up, as he says: "So's you can turn a tidy profit when your time comes."

Now that the deal is all but done, he begins to regard me with less suspicion and more affection, but it's manly all the while, somewhere between buddy-buddy and father-son. It's clear that I barely understand the difference between a Phillips and a flathead screwdriver, never mind soffit versus fascia. Because I don't know what he's talking about, he's having to come up with tortuous definitions of simple things, like molding ("that sort of carved, long strip of wood where the floor meets the wall") and joists ("that piece of wood right there — the one my hand is on").

"You remind me of my boy, Stanley Jr.," he says, giving up. "He just don't have a mind for work. Doesn't know one end of a hammer from the other 'less I hit him with it." He sighs affectionately.

"My boy, you know, he's into the physics. I just can't keep my mind around it to follow more than two or three words into anything he's saying. But I guess somebody else does, because he's going to England, you know, in Europe, for an internship this summer."

He shakes his head and stares at his tennis shoes for a second. He pronounces England like *Ingleland*.

I tell him that he must be very proud.

"I am," he says. "They're paying his way! Can you believe that? And do you know what he's going for? To study — get this — glass."

"Glass?" I say. I think Stanley has already equated the fact that I teach at a college with the fact that his son is in college and concluded that we must know each other. There can't be that many of us.

He wipes the sweat from his mustache with his hand and then wipes that on the pocket that hangs below the shaggy hem of his short shorts. "Glass," he says.

Before I know it an hour has come and gone, and he has told me all about the small but prestigious private college in Iowa his boy goes to, how he got into the sciences and was always lapping his classmates when it came to doing those equations and so forth, and before anybody knew which way was up, his professors were asking him to teach their classes. And now some "lady perfesser" from Ingleland wants him to come over to help them work on glass. As if everybody doesn't know what glass is already.

Sully begins to get really busy right after Stanley accepts our offer. Some new development is expanding south of the city, and the lots alone are going for a quarter of a million dollars. Through one of his improv/missionary connections, Sully is among the few realtors who gets to sell the properties. Within a week he has four offers pending. Granted, his take is only around two percent, because of the way the developers wrote it up, but we're talking two percent of million-dollar homes. That's like twenty grand apiece. Suddenly he isn't working at the restaurant and it has become impossible to reach anything but his voice mail.

The inspection comes and goes without event, but we don't know what the bottom line is until days later, when Sully brings the big binder to the restaurant for me. I leaf through it without finding a complete sentence in the lot. It's a plastic-covered thesaurus of lawyer gibberish. The comments range from "issues of aesthetics in most rooms," "furnace signs of age," and "might not be or seem not to be sufficient," to "shed rust in backyard" and "finding rust compromising."

"What the hell are we supposed to do with this?" I ask him. The inspection cost three hundred dollars. Far as I can tell, the inspector put equal emphasis on the framing and the feline miasma seeping from the carpet.

Sully smiles and fake-punches me in the arm. "Ees bueno, my freend. Ees all very, how do dju say, goot." He scoops a handful of anise mints from the hostess's desk.

We don't know what we are doing, buying this house, and are depending on a little expertise somewhere along the way. "Sully, it doesn't say a goddamned thing that makes sense."

Sully bobbles his head back and forth as he stabilizes his personae. "Okay," he says, "all right."

"Did you read it?"

"Hey, all right," he says. "I looked at it." He unwraps and then rewraps a mint. "I mean, I'll look at it."

When he calls a couple of days later, without elaboration, I get really upset. We are supposed to close on the house in a few days, and Sully is going to be in San Diego on vacation.

"Sully," I say, "I'm not sure what your job is right now, but Jenae and I don't feel like you're exactly being all you can be." I can't believe myself. I am becoming that guy. "I'm a freaking English teacher, Sully, and all I can make out of this report is that this guy is basically throwing around cold, wet pasta at us. It doesn't mean anything to me, and it's not supposed to. Is that what we paid him for, to tell us nothing in as offensive yet meaningless a way as possible? If you want to help us out, read the report tonight and figure out what the hell it says and if we're supposed to do something about anything or not."

The next day, Sully makes a list of things for Stanley to do before closing and faxes it to him and copies it to Jenae and me. They are all of the things that have concerned us but we don't know anything about. Things like "bathroom GFCI outlet ground not verified." We don't know if this requires pushing a button or hiring an electrician to rewire the house.

Stanley doesn't make a big deal out of any of our requests and promises he'll have them all fixed up, but it is embarrassing and exposes our real, raw ignorance. What's the risk of an improperly grounded outlet or a poorly sistered stud? We don't know and nobody is telling us anything other than "Don't worry." But all we hear is the last word. Worry worry *worry*.

When the day of the closing arrives, we find Stanley already at the title company with his youngest son, Stanley III, who looks like a smaller version of himself, right down to the short-short jean shorts.

Like the inspector and the realtor, the title or "abstract" company did something inexplicable that costs a lot of money. The place smells, feels, and looks like an orthodontist's office and features inspirational photos of birds of prey on the walls, with semi-socialist words below them like "teamwork" and "dedication."

A tall blond woman wearing a tight, low-cut tank top minces her way into the reception area, flips her hair over her shoulders like a pole dancer, and smiles at Stanley and Stanley III. "Gentlemen," she says.

"Ma'am," Stanley says. Stanley III puts his hands in his lap.

She places a basket of individually wrapped cookies and chips on the glass table.

"Please do help yourself," she says, as though there's another way they are usually dispensed.

She takes Stanley and his son into an adjoining room to have a seller's chat, and Jenae and I try not to get stuck to the vinyl couch. It doesn't feel like the big day it is supposed to be. In fact, it feels like things can go south at a moment's notice and we'll be living out of Jenae's Beetle instead of moving into a home of our own.

"Chips Ahoy?" Jenae offers. "For that special occasion?"

"Don't mind if I do."

The abstract woman comes to get us and brings with her a spiky-haired man in a cardigan, braces, and a Bluetooth headset who is, from what I can gather, talking to his orthodontist. He waves to us but stares into that alternate dimension where people look while they're on the phone.

"He's your Sully for the day," the woman says.

Stanley nods toward the snack basket. "Those really free?"

"Only today," she says. She spreads her fingers across the glass table as if she has just painted her nails and is either really proud of them or afraid of smearing the wet polish. They are, all ten of them, little American flags. "Ready set go?"

"Heck yes," Stanley says. Stanley III is staring at the woman's cleavage.

Jenae and I nod meekly.

Our substitute Sully is still on the phone. We look at him for direction.

"Oh, hey, yeah," he says. "Go get 'em." He gives us a big thumbs-up.

2

Execute ye judgment and righteousness,
and deliver the spoiled out of the hand
of the oppressor, and do no wrong . . .
If ye will not hear these words, I swear
by myself, saith the Lord, that this house
shall become a desolation.

— JEREMIAH 22

Gathering Jacks

WE ARE ON 13th East, northbound, stuck in traffic on a Sunday, not quite arguing about where we are going to eat. One of us is talking about how fat we are. How fat we have become. It could have been either of us. It isn't really true.

My grandma has been dead for four months. Cases of cheap domestic beer and vials of Viagra now litter my grandfather's condo. When he isn't with Ruth in Indianapolis, he's with Tonya in Hales Corners, on the rough south side of Milwaukee. He has just sort of bought us a house, though, and that is supposed to make it all better. It wasn't the first house we really wanted. It wasn't even the second house we really wanted. It was the first house we didn't really want but thought we could get. It feels a little like a loss, and we have a hell of a lot of work to do that is well beyond our ken.

The sun is brutalizing us in Jenae's VW. There is a lot of traffic for a Sunday morning, when, because everyone is in church, only tumbleweeds and apostates freely roam the streets. We drive to our new house and go right on by. In a clear plastic cup the keys sit, like all the leftover ones from the junk drawer we lack the confidence to throw away, fearing they are the only way to open something unremembered and locked.

We are having the low-blood-sugar conversation we tend to have on Sunday mornings. The not pretty talk tinged with mild hangovers and the concussive August sun. Food is all anybody ever wanted. Food and shelter. But we are fat, somebody is saying. And we have a house we don't particularly know what to do with. We certainly don't want to go inside it again without a plan and some masks.

In the lane next to ours is a guy on a Kawasaki Ninja, his left turn signal pulsing almost in time with the throbbing in my temples. He has tattoos up and down both his arms, but I can only see the right one, close to us, which seems to be decorated with a tribal design. In front of the Ninja guy is a minivan, and he keeps craning his neck, trying to see around it, though there's nothing to see, just the empty light-rail tracks and a red traffic signal.

I am rapt by the Ninja guy's tattoos. But the problem with tattoos is that they're on somebody's body, at which one is generally not met with equanimity for staring. Even beautiful people tend to discourage onlookers from staring at their forearms or chests or what have you for more than a glance. But try not looking at someone's tattoo. You can't do it. You can't not look. And then you feel — even if you don't like what you see — a bit jealous. I could get a tattoo, you think. But I probably won't, you admit. Or you'll get, as I did one lame spring break, a little star on your ankle, at which the tattoo artist, Lou, in my case, will scoff at you and say, "Shit, I'll have you in and out of here like a wedding dick on a honeymoon," and it all will have been somehow worthwhile. A mistake, to be sure, but one with a story and at least a hint of decisiveness. Usually, after all, we don't get to choose our scars.

Most of us — like my wife and I — can't even decide where we want to have one stupid meal on one stupid Sunday morning. Breakfast food? Brunch food? Should we pick someplace popular like Ruth's, where the waitlist is long enough so that by the time we'd be seated we could have breakfast or lunch? Or should we slum it at the International House of Pancakes with all the letter-jacket jocks and their freshly deflowered girlfriends wearing awkward prescription glasses because their eyes are too puffy to get their contacts in? There's always the Training Table, which was locally famous for having, instead of table service, phones at each table — a concept popular with, well, no one, but they make up for it in bacon. Or if you're in the mood to hang out with the polygamists who can't resist bringing all the kids and wives for the onion rings and fry sauce (a local abomination of roughly equal parts ketchup and mayonnaise), then Hires Big H drive-in is definitely the place.

Good or bad, even this guy on the Ninja has made some decisions, and his body is the proof. I wonder what I would look like with a bunch of tattoos, snaking up and down my arms like the result of a bad breakup or a threat made good. His look something like lightning, something like smoke.

Jenae and I are silent. Nevertheless, we have settled on lunch at B & D Burgers by campus. I never suggest it; she never asks for it. It's an understood default. If you've got the stomach, they've got the zucchini fries, and it's guaranteed to be Mormon-free on a Sunday morning because the most people they can seat at any table is four, and, well, it's Sunday. The place is just the other side of 5th South, and we are practically there.

Salt Lake Sundays, when you're not a Mormon, make you feel a bit like a refugee. You sort of wander around, not really having a handle on the language or the customs, but knowing enough to recognize the signs you should stay away from. Places that say "Visitors Welcome" but don't say when. Places that say "A Family Favorite" but have baroque-framed pictures of horrifying presidents in the window. Places that say "A Utah Original." Places where the parking lot looks like a conversion-van dealership.

The rest of the week you can pretend you live somewhere else. Stay close to the English department. Watch cable TV. Read the *New York Times* — especially the Dining and Wine section, which in local papers would be Buffet and Pop. Shop at adult bookstores. Drink imported (meaning regular-strength) beer. Smoke. For what it's worth, all you have to do to make yourself anathema in Utah is drink coffee. Hell, regular Coke would pretty much do. All are strictly verboten in the Mormon Church.

I always work at the restaurant on Saturday nights, and after toiling for eight or ten nonstop hours at culinary hostage negotiations, I'm always amped up until two or three in the morning. By the time I get home I need a drink and some time and space to just sit and watch *Austin City Limits* or *Antiques Roadshow*. Without gin and PBS, I'm not sure anybody would survive working in a restaurant and waking up in Salt Lake City.

After lunch, rather than CD or shoe shopping, we plan on hitting the renovation stores for ideas. Instead of going to places where we would need to remind aggressively indifferent teenagers that they were at work, we go to where adults skilled in trades would dare us to do the same. Appliance stores. Carpet stores. Hardware stores. Stores that sell the stuff with which you make other stores. Stores that are so big they have different climate zones. Stores that have more raw than finished material being trucked around by kamikaze forklift operators. It's not every store where you can get killed if the merchandise falls on you.

* * *

In light of the "aesthetic issues" the inspector has pointed out (as though they aren't as apparent as sunlight in a mineshaft), we have decided to basically gut the house. We are throwing out the old carpet/litter box. The avocado stove and refrigerator. The asbestos-flavored, paisley-patterned linoleum. The imitation knotty pine glued-on veneer cabinet doors. The imitation knotty pine glued-on veneer walls. The margarine-colored, faux brass-accented plastic countertop. The marigold-painted tinfoil shed out back. The rusted-through water heater featuring an exposed flame. The small oil refinery they once called a furnace that takes up the entire basement. That's for starters. We don't know where — *if* — it will end.

I like to think of myself as something of an expert consumer. That is, when I set out to buy something, I try to do as my grandma taught me: buy the best once. Of course, I know as she did that there is rarely a product that is hands down the best for everyone, everywhere. But I can usually figure out what that means for me.

Not so with the house. Not in Salt Lake anyway. Other cities might have services to help consumers, but in Salt Lake everybody gets the skinny at church. There are no other options. You can't just pick up *Consumer Reports* to figure out what the best HVAC people are in your area. What you can tell is who advertises the most, who drives the most conspicuous vans, and who has the most of what they call "Big Sales Events" but appear to be their perpetual jacked-up-then-superficially-slashed prices. But you also quickly realize that no matter who you eventually contract to do the work or deliver the goods, there is a whole netherworld of subcontractors and sub-subcontractors that drive the pedophile-ready, ratty-but-anonymous white IRA vans with the tinted windows and stickers hailing long-dead stock-car martyrs.

We soon find ourselves adrift in a shopping world where it is virtually impossible to tell what you are going to get from whom. But that doesn't stop us from shopping around and making arbitrary decisions based not on research and analysis but rather on fatigue and heat exhaustion.

We have a month left on our lease. We figure that will be plenty of time. Still waiting for the light to turn green, Jenae makes a partial list. All we need to do in a month is:

1. Pack
2. Change locks
3. Replace some carpet
4. Tear up the rest
5. Replace meth-stained light fixtures
6. Replace cabinets
7. Replace sink (just the kitchen one — the bathroom one is all right)
8. Replace appliances
9. Do *something* about the countertop
10. Replace furnace
11. Replace water heater
12. Tear down shed
13. Replace garage door
14. Dig out old "garden" (stumps and dirt piled against garage door)
15. Replace windows
16. Replace kitchen floor
17. Sand the hardwoods
18. Worry about laundry room
19. Paint

and, of course,

20. Move.

We have roughly thirty days to take care of that list before our lease is up. And shop for all of the above. And work full time. And we don't even know what to do about lunch.

I still can't make out the tattoos on the guy on the motorcycle, so I nose an inch closer to the car in front of us. The guy keeps twisting his throttle, flexing and tensing his forearm. The minivan in front of him blocks his view and he seems eager to get around it.

The light finally changes and they get the green arrow to turn left, and he twists his throttle and kicks his bike into gear while we wait for our own light to go straight. Everybody in the two turning lanes eases forward, and suddenly both lanes light up with brake lights and the guy on the bike nearly goes over his handlebars he stops so fast. He settles back down and it isn't clear what's going on because the drivers can see that they have the green arrow. And then I hear what I could swear is a doorbell, and Jenae says something, and I haven't had any coffee yet and I just want to be out of the car so I can eat my freaking hamburger and zucchini fries and maybe a butterscotch shake and gird up and go to the goddamned Home Depot.

And then I see it: the Trax light-rail train. The left-turning car is flying through the intersection without any apparent intent or ability to stop. "Oh my God," Jenae says, and the minivan in front of the motorcycle keeps turning left downhill, kind of gunning it but not nearly fast enough — it's turning — turning away from the train coming from uphill and to our right and the train is finally braking but that obviously isn't going to work in time, sparks or not, and in a second nothing is going to matter at all. The train rings its cheery bell again but it's far too late for anybody to do anything.

Jenae throws her face into her hands as though we are the ones about to be hit.

Two years ago, I saw an accident that involved a couple of fairly slow-moving cars. It was a head-on collision, but the turning car wasn't even moving five miles an hour and the driver of the on-coming car was able to slam on his brakes so that the impact was abrupt but minimal. It was the most beautiful thing I'd ever seen.

The glass from the headlights exploded into the air, and for just a second, though I was passing in the curb lane traveling at thirty miles an hour, everything was perfectly still. There was no other traffic, no sound. It was as if time had been momentarily gathered in the space of that collision, like a pair of jacks in a fist, and nothing moved. The air spun slowly with the finest particles of glass blown from the pulverized headlights. The cars bowed into each other, head to head, their rear tires lifted slightly off the ground, the only things spinning.

And then the jacks dropped, and then came the concussion of metal and air bags and the horns and the screeching. But for a single moment it was sublime. It was terrible. It was beautiful. I didn't want to be in awe, but I was.

The train, however, strikes the minivan between the passenger side front and rear doors and pushes it from the middle of the intersection fifty feet downhill. The train has this rectangular metal front bumper about the size of a filing cabinet, and it rams the van precisely in the middle of the door so that it can't slide off or around but instead stays mounted right there on the front of that train like its own hood ornament.

They finally stop, the car sloughs off the bumper, and then nothing happens. Because of the glare, I can't see the conductor or any of the passengers, but I don't think any of them would have been hurt — it was a nice, gradual stop for them. I imagine some of them must have seen the van, especially the conductor, perched atop five hundred tons of metal and flesh as it approached what was essentially a family packaged in a bento box.

The tattooed guy drops his motorcycle, throws his helmet to the ground, and runs to the scene. Jenae smothers her face in her hands as though it's on fire. People in the cars around us are getting out, peering over their roofs like prairie dogs, dialing their cell phones. I am frozen. I don't have a phone with me. I don't know any emergency techniques other than the Heimlich, and it is clear that more than that is going to be necessary. The motorcycle helmet spins, empty, on the pavement.

Now the driver jumps out of the minivan. She faces the back door and, for an instant, does nothing; she seems to be waiting for her understanding to catch up with her body.

And then I realize that I just can't hear her. She *is* doing something. She is screaming. She begins to tear at her long hair, jumping up and down, stamping the road as if to shake it back in time. "My babies," she screams. That's what she's saying. "My babies. My babies."

I steer around the clotted traffic and drive onto campus and stop the car. I pull Jenae from where she has slumped against the dashboard and hold her until we hear the ambulance.

I had no idea how spoiled I was, no idea I still have so much to lose. I had no idea that I could lose that which I didn't even yet have.

I need to get my shit together, I realize. We aren't going to get another chance.

The Mandoor

$*$ $*$ $*$

JENAE'S DAD, LEE, and his wife, Diane, have come out to
Utah for an agriculture convention. They are busy with meetings
and sightseeing, but they make it a point to take us out to dinner
and, of course, want to see the house.

Lee is a third-generation Republican River valley farmer in
south-central Nebraska. The first time I visited their home, Lee
was out by the Quonset with Jenae's two younger brothers, John
and Tyler. They were changing the transmission on an Oldsmobile
and each had his own pair of pliers. They seemed painfully incon-
venienced to have to put them down in order to crush my little
croissant of a hand. Afterward, the brothers said nothing, picked
up their pliers, and went back to their work. Before disappearing
under the hood, Lee took me in for a few more seconds from behind his large tinted glasses.

"You're from Wisconsin," he said. "Good soil from what I gather.
Hunting too."

I looked to Jenae, who was beaming at her father. She was so
proud to have me visit and meet her family and see her land that
she was blinded to the fact that no one here at home was exactly
eager for her to get involved with an East Coast English major
who was likely a fairy.

"And cows," I said. It was a stretch, but I knew I had to stand my ground. I was reasonably certain I could back up my assertion.

I expected some kind of interrogation or hazing ritual featuring a car battery, chain-link fencing, and my face, but instead Lee worked his pliers a couple of times and gestured back toward his boys.

Despite our somewhat chilly first meeting, I have seen nothing but sweetness from Lee. Though he might not have been the husband his first wife wanted him to be, in the years I have come to know him, he has been a guileless, gentle, and almost recklessly generous man who cannot enter a gift shop, truck stop, or co-op without garnering Cornhusker tchotchkes, Remington commemorative knife sets, and his-and-hers Black Hills gold rings for his children, me included.

Before Diane and Lee got married and bought a new double-wide to park permanently at the farm, she was living with her kids in a house that had been built around a trailer. When her father was finished with all but the last wall, he hooked his tractor to the trailer and dragged it out. That must have been something.

"Let's go see the house!" Lee says when we pick them up at their downtown hotel. They have just returned from a visit to the Bingham Canyon Mine, west of Salt Lake City, which is essentially a huge hole in the shape of an upside-down mountain. They are ready to be impressed again, and more than a little curious to see what so much money can buy. The hundred fifty grand we've paid for Stanley's house could have bought an entire block in the town of Orleans, where they are from, or close to a hundred acres of farmland. The house Jenae grew up in has been appraised recently at thirty-two thousand. Most farmers' trucks cost more than their homes. As far as most Nebraskans are concerned, the only reason to spend a hundred fifty thousand dollars is a twelve-row combine or a clone of Tom Osborne.

"All right," Jenae says before she lets them in, "keep in mind that we're going to be doing a lot of work, okay?"

"Sure, honey," Diane says. "Remember, we live on a farm, for the love of God."

"Well," Jenae says, stepping aside, "this is different. At least you can eat the things that grow on a farm."

Lee gives Jenae a squeeze. "Come on, sis," he says. I love that he calls her sis, but I don't really understand it. "Don't be silly," he says. "Nothing could be that bad. We're just so proud of you two. Your own house!"

We are back outside in under two minutes. The smell is so bad with the day's heat and the windows shut that they didn't even go into the bedroom or office. "I'm sure they're just as — nice," Lee says, "as the — rest of the place."

Diane is doubled over, rifling through her purse for cigarettes or anything to burn and inhale. "And I thought mine was a pit," Diane says. "Jesus, kids. I hope you guys know what you're doing."

Lee takes off his glasses and wipes his eyes. "That's some smell," he says. "Makes the feedlot seem like a flower shop."

Not long after, Debby, Jenae's mom, as well as her boyfriend, Ed, and her grandparents come out to help us tidy up. They were all loaded into Debby's Chrysler, with Ed at the helm and Grandpa George riding shotgun. It's a big, late-model American car, but with Ed standing only four foot ten, even with lifts in his cowboy boots he has to sit with pillows beneath and behind him in order to reach the pedals. Grandpa George, on the other hand, at over three hundred pounds is so big each one of his limbs is as big as Ed.

"Get me the hell out of here," Grandma Carol Ann yells as Ed slows to a stop. She is shoehorned behind her husband, holding an orange cooler the size of a small refrigerator on her lap. A young and energetic grandma, she pops out from the rear door like a cheerleader. "That man," she says, pointing back at Ed, "is a menace. Jenae, do you have any iced tea for your poor old grandma?"

Ed is still parking the car, driving slowly back and forth in the rough vicinity of the curb. In rural Nebraska, you can drive your entire life without ever shifting into reverse, never mind parallel parking.

"Goddamn it, Edward!" George says. "I've got to goddamned urinate here."

"That's not the half of it," Grandma Carol Ann says. She drops into a chair on our porch and rocks herself nervously. "It's the bungee cords."

Jenae and I look at each other. "Bungee cords?"

"The bungee cords!" Carol Ann resumes. "Driving eighty miles an hour down the interstate, doing just fine as you please, when he sees a bungee cord and jumps on the brake and all of a sudden you're thrown into the back of your husband's head. Probably did that a hundred times. I'll kill him, that's all. I'll kill him the next time he so much as lets off the gas for one."

"You say that now," Ed says, ambling around the front of the car, immensely proud of his big-city parking job. "But there'll come a day, by God, when you need one — hit a deer, say, and want to take it home for the meat — and what are you gonna use to lash it to the hood? Grandpa's belt, maybe, but short of that, you'll be high and dry."

"I heard that, Edward." Grandpa George is preparing to extricate himself from the passenger seat. He's such a large man it appears that the car has been built around him. "Not very goddamned funny," he says, "never you mind the fact that I don't wear a belt with my overalls. Come over here and give me a hand so I can pummel the ever living shit out of you."

Debby walks right past me, kisses Jenae on the cheek, and goes inside. "I need to lie down," she says.

They are here to help. It is going to be interesting.

"Matthew," Ed says from below, shaking my hand Napoleonically hard, "do you have any idea what they charge for bungee cords at Bosselman's? You'd never believe it, so you might as well go ahead and guess."

We drive Debby and Carol Ann to the house and fix them up with ripped T-shirts they can use for face masks, and they set about the unenviable task of cleaning the bathroom. Jenae and I are going to spend our first night in the house, so her family can sleep in our apartment. Despite the massive amount of work that lies ahead of us, little of it can be done before the carpet is torn up, and as most surfaces are going to be taken down to bare wood, there isn't that much for them to do. Nonetheless, after nearly two hours they have exhausted all our cleaning supplies and have to go to the store to re-up, leaving me alone with George and Ed.

We have specific instructions to come up with a project that doesn't involve exotic dancers or anything else that will get Ed's angina up or blow out Grandpa's knee. The women aren't sure that either of them — never mind me — has any home renovation skills left in them. Ed fancies himself a jack of all trades, based on the premise that if one can install hydraulic hay bale lifts on stake-body pickups, then one can do just about anything. He is also an aspiring masseur, aromatherapist, RV deliveryman, and soon-to-be Internet debt collector.

"Got to stay diversified," Ed says, and he does, with respect to both work and women. He is an immensely likable man who would do anything you asked of him so long as it doesn't come with too tight a time frame. He lives with his father, two hours away from Debby in North Platte. They met while country swing dancing, in which he is regionally famous for his ability to whip around women several times his own body weight. He is so popular that the only break he gets from dancing all night is to sneak out to his truck to change his sweat-soaked shirt. In a state where the only way you can get men on the dance floor is to tell them that there are Oklahoma Sooner fans hitting on their women, a guy like Ed is a hot commodity.

Grandpa George clearly thinks that Debby is wasting her time with a man as diminutive as Ed — barely big enough to serve as one of his own meals — but George used to play accordion at the dances back when his body could handle it, so they have an appreciation for similar things. And when you factor in Grandpa's taste for the "dancers" at the Tower Nite Club up in Holdrege, they make as good a pair as tomato juice and beer — the unofficial state drink. George has been "retired" for years following a suspicious electrical fire that leveled a warehouse he was working on, so while Carol Ann checks bags at the grocery store, he spends his days fooling around online with classic-car chat rooms and soft-core amateur porn, but in his heart he is still a workingman. He had, after all, built their house in Oxford, Nebraska. He also jacked it up to add a basement and later replaced the entire roof himself. It wasn't his fault that the meteorologists failed to predict that one of the worst storms in Furnass County history would strike when his house had the top down. Water flowed from their ceiling fan for days.

Given their collective résumé, I decide to pick a project that can succeed or fail with little consequence.

Our garage has two doors. When Stanley showed me the place,

he gestured from the backyard at the free-standing structure. "Garage door works good," he said. "Don't know if you can put an opener in it on account of the double header I've got in there for swapping out the transmissions me and Dad used to do on the side. The mandoor, on the other hand, is gonna need a little work."

I wasn't sure I had heard him correctly.

"Mandoor?" I said. I thought it might be a neighborhood gay bar. In Boston, I lived around the corner from a place called the Ramrod. Anything was possible.

"I know," Stanley said. "It's pretty bad, buried as it is behind that sorry excuse for a rose bush the tenant lady tried to plant there. Guess she didn't want nobody using that entrance, come up and give her a scare."

I assumed a thoughtful pose.

Stanley shook his head at my denseness.

"The door," he said. "Right there. The other door the garage's got. Not the garage door. The *man*door."

And sure enough, there was indeed a door — a mandoor — on the side of the garage. The whole wall of the building was faded to the shade of driftwood and buried up to my knee in dirt, and some sort of wizened vegetation stood in front of a door that was no better for wear, the bottom panel rotted through and the other two not far behind.

Here is a project we could tackle like men, but with no real risk of disappointment, I think, because even failure will look better than what was already there. Then again, that described most of the house.

At the hardware store, what with George's immense heft and bad knees, he was getting set to use one of the orange scooters with a shopping cart wired to the handlebars, but we lose him first to the lunch counter near the entrance, which is tended by a haggard but bikini-clad woman who taps her cigarette ashes into the hot-dog water.

That leaves Ed and me to do the shopping. Fortunately, there aren't a lot of options in the mandoor department. It's pretty much white or almond, left- or right-side knob. They come already attached to a frame and so, theoretically, you're supposed to be able to simply measure it up and slip it right on in. That is my hope, anyway, as we drive back to our house with a door strapped to the roof of Debby's Chrysler, praying to the gods of the highway that we won't cross paths with any errant bungee cords.

"Now, goddamn it, Edward," Grandpa George says, "how's a man supposed to tell you what to do if you keep getting in his light?"

Grandpa sits on a folding metal chair that shrieks under his weight as he points with his cane and grunts commands at Ed and me. We have gotten the old door out just by trying to open it; it disintegrated into a pile of kindling and left a ragged but vaguely door-shaped hole in the wall.

"It don't measure the same at the top and bottom," Ed says. He stands on an overturned bucket like the conductor of a street corner orchestra.

"Well, I can goddamned see that, Edward," Grandpa says. "We're gonna have to cut a bigger hole is what we're gonna have to do."

"We are indeed," Ed says. "Give me that Sawzall there, Matthew."

I comply, but not without a quiet prayer first.

After a few minutes of eyeballing his line, Ed cuts a hole roughly double the size of the new door. Fortunately for us, Stanley has squirreled away in the garage a great supply of old, oily scrap wood, which Grandpa proceeds to throw at Ed. Eventually, we manage to get a new frame within an inch or so of fitting the prehung door.

"Got any screws sitting around here?" Grandpa asks. "Real long ones?"

By the time we finish, the door is spiked and riddled with three-inch-long screws and shims, and a halo of light shines around the new frame, but the thing opens and closes, and one by one we walk through it and pronounce it "close enough for country music" and go to find our ceremonial Pabst Blue Ribbons, even though we have finished far from first place.

This Little Knife of Mine

MICHAEL, OUR NEIGHBOR in the house next to our apartment, is working in his garage, building a desk for his granddaughter. He smokes a pipe and wears white painter's coveralls and has a long white beard. He is patient, great with kids, always remembers Maggie's name, and if there were ever any shortage of apostles, Michael, I am confident, would make a fine substitute.

Michael is working with a wood-turning machine, peeling away locks of bright white wood to reveal a purple vein beneath. Clearly, he is a professional. He has tools that I have never seen and could not name, never mind turn on or operate. Smoke from cherry pipe tobacco and fresh sawdust waft around like an elixir to cure things from which you didn't know you were suffering.

The carpet installers are supposed to be at the house any minute, but I stop to chat with Michael first. To spurn someone like Michael is to beg misfortune. We need his handyman's luck. Already we're behind. We wanted to do a whole slew of things before the carpet came up — like sand the cottage cheese texture off the walls, then prime and paint so we could use the old carpet as a dropcloth — but we couldn't decide on colors, and we forgot why we wanted to paint before we sanded the floors, so we didn't.

Michael hands me a piece of blood-red wood. It's heavy and

dense as a bar of precious metal. "Purpleheart," he says. "That's what it's called."

He has cut the purpleheart down to a one-by-one-inch board and glued maple planks around it to make a rough square leg for the desk. He mounts the leg horizontally on the turning machine — called a lathe, he says — and while it rotates like an axle he uses a set of long-handled chisels and knives to peel and shape the wood into a nicely curved leg. Blond maple curls pile up on the floor like lost ringlets in a wig factory.

I ask him where he got the wood, the purpleheart.

"Macbeth's," he says.

I repeat the name, and he nods. If he doubts that I have any need for a specialty lumber store named after that Scottish king with blood-stained hands, he doesn't betray it.

I actually have got wood on my mind, since the carpet guy will be at the house any minute and we'll finally see what the floor is really made of. I had asked Stanley to show me what was beneath the carpet, but he said he couldn't tear it up in case our deal fell through and "the Oriental" still wanted it. "She was real into the carpet," he had said.

We had shopped and shopped for the bedroom and study carpeting, but until you install a carpet on a couple hundred square feet of floor, all you see are placemat-size remnants like you sat on in kindergarten. I'm afraid we'll get it down and then hate it. I know this couple who stayed at the Marriott and ate every meal at my restaurant for six weeks while they had their kitchen remodeled — twice, because they didn't like the first renovation. We don't quite have that luxury. The more we do ourselves, the more we can afford to do. Carpet, however, is not something I am going to fabricate, and installation is free where we shopped, so for the first interior project I get to be the benign overseer.

We weren't sure how much carpet we'd end up buying. There appeared to be hardwood under the living and dining room carpet, but beyond that, we didn't know. The bedroom and the study felt spongy, but that could have been due to a lot of padding or a couple of layers of carpet on top of each other. All in all, it just didn't seem worth it. Carpet is nice. The pets would like carpet. Everybody could sleep on the floor. Carpet is for lovers, for families. And weevils, I suppose.

Me, I don't care much for carpet because I don't like vacuum cleaners — they scare Maggie, and she tends to be right about stuff that scares her. For example, she doesn't like cars. What percentage of car rides result in dog-oriented destinations? Practically none. Another example: she *likes* mail carriers. They wear shorts and black socks and pith helmets and know where you live and see your mail and therefore know who cares about you and where your money goes. It is good to be kind to people like that. She is a smart dog.

The carpet, however, was beyond me. Even though I was resistant, I had to be a part of the process. Participation is the sine qua non of marriage. And after seeing that train hit that car the other day, and what with all the loss and illness looming around us, I wanted to be better at being married, because, after all, I was, and it's sad when people don't try to be better at who they are. One way to be better at being married, of course, is by contributing. That means taking a stand on things as though they were of immense importance to you. Such as: the kind, tightness, weave, warp and weft of carpet as it pertains to one's own aesthetic sensibility and a house's potential resale value, as well as durability and overall quality of life. Although I hate math and think the word "algorithm" sounds like a Havana fusion jazz band, I prayed for an equation to make this easier. I sought high and low for any kind of solution, but all the guides and websites and hymnals just told me to follow my heart. And I tried.

I'm mostly colorblind, and in carpet stores — like paint stores — you've got all of these little samples and, from them, you're supposed to be able to imagine the whole surface covered with the junk. It would be like a car dealer having no cars, just the keys — a whole room filled with racks and racks of keys — and you base your purchase of a car on extrapolating what kind of vehicle would fit on the end of each key.

So, to be a good sport and to keep things interesting for myself, I decide I'll cast my vote based on the carpet's name. Not unheard of in any democracy, of course.

Monsanto, I think. Mohawk. Good, strong names. Like scouts in a James Fenimore Cooper novel. Berber? No. It makes my mouth feel regrettable. Also rhymes with Gerber, which is baby food, which you don't want to walk on barefoot. Stainmaster? Yes. You bet your ass I want carpet that has an advanced degree in something. Doctor of Pile. Master of Stains. That's my kind of carpet.

Suffice it to say, Jenae quickly pooh-poohed this approach, and we decided that the best way to choose carpet and remain married was for her to pick the bedroom and me the study. If I wanted to continue sleeping in the bedroom, she gently reminded me, I had better choose wisely in the study.

So I went conservative. And Jenae? She went Brady. She went *really* Brady. Three-inch-deep-shag Brady. If we were to have a Grateful Dead party — and I'm not saying it's impossible, but a pretty long list of other things would have to happen first; for example, number one: start liking the Dead — we could have a black light installed in our bedroom and everybody could groove on the wavy forest of mighty white worms dancing on the floor. In the daylight, however, the sample from the carpet store looked like a scalped ram.

On the other hand, because the study was ostensibly a common space, I decided on high-wear, semi-commercial, tight-weave, beige/brown/khaki carpet. So, she got to pick out the dancing shoes, I got to pick out the orthopedic insoles. The stuff I chose was the color of toast and had about the same underfoot feel. But I was secretly planning this mild-mannered carpet to be my means of a discrete triumph, because, let me tell you, I eat a hell of a lot of toast while I'm working, and I'm pretty reckless with my crumb management.

After leaving Michael to his ministry upon the purpleheart, I wander around the inside of the house, waiting for the carpet guy. I try not to touch anything. Everything feels sticky, as though booger-smearing had been the previous tenants' favorite pastime — right up there with home-brewing meth or crack, I dread. I open all the windows I can, but it still smells of ammonia, fecal matter, and, if I'm not mistaken, star anise — like the backed-up septic system of an Indian restaurant. I'm sure it'll all be better with new floors. New carpet. The end of the day, this place is going to be a whole new house. That's my story. I keep telling it to myself, taking shallow breaths to stave off hyperventilation and despair.

I don't have any tools, per se, other than a starter-model Swiss Army knife — one without a saw or corkscrew, but with tweezers, a plastic toothpick, and the oft-sought Phillips screwdriver — and for three hours I try to slice through the decades of paint that have sealed the bedroom windows closed. It is a demoralizing first project. If I can't even get the windows open, what will I be able to do?

The carpet guy finally shows up around eleven. I expect him to say something — to comment on how fit and righteous I must be to have been up for hours, busy as I am with my little red knife — but he doesn't.

"We're gonna have to do something about the smell," he says. "Get these suckers open," he says, as though he's going to say *Ali Baba!* and the windows will pop right up.

He is wearing a short-sleeved blue mechanic's jumpsuit, and the name "LaEarl" is stitched in a white oval patch. He seems at home in his jumpsuit. I am willing to bet he has a few of these and that he wears them everywhere except funerals. The waistband has a built-in belt that I do not understand. It is a jumpsuit. The belt is, I believe, pure fanciness. There is no chance the jumpsuit will fall from his shoulders, off his arms and torso, over his hips, and down. A belt on a jumpsuit is more redundant than a belt with suspenders. A belt on a jumpsuit is like lederhosen with suspenders and a belt. Perhaps he thinks the ladies like it.

LaEarl looks like my seventh-grade wood shop teacher, Mr. Hruska, not to be confused with my eighth-grade metal shop teacher, Mr. Tonz, who threw a roll of duct tape at my friend Joseph's head and called him a "stupid homo" because he was talking during attendance. Shop teachers all have gray, G.I. Joe flattops, thick Lucite glasses, and an inordinate amount of ear and nose hair. Men who look like that are good at one thing, it seems to me, and it is not interpersonal communication. It is their work. And sadism.

Through the window I can see LaEarl's rusty, failing blue

pickup. One taillight appears to have been stolen from a school bus, because it is big, round, and red, mounted by the gas tank like a pencil sharpener. The new carpet is rolled up in twelve-foot tubes, wrapped in plastic like huge carryout burritos. It occurs to me that he might have stolen them from somebody else's legitimate carpet company truck, but then I remember that I ordered the carpet, and unless he stole both the carpet and the order — as well as the money I have not yet paid — he would be doing me a tremendous favor.

"Fixer-upper," he says, looking around, wrinkling his nose.

"How can you tell?" I ask. I don't expect him to answer. It is not necessary to answer. Olfaction is forty times more receptive than any other human sense.

"Good grief," he says.

"A little incense and a coat of paint or two . . ." I say, looking around as if I'm about to be lowered down a reasonably deep well.

"Where you want me to start?" he asks.

For a second, I am confused. I have never employed anybody before. I have never before had anybody perform manual labor that required my oversight. I suddenly feel I should be wearing a straw boater, sipping a mint julep, and fiddling absent-mindedly with my riding crop.

I don't want LaEarl to think I'm some kind of schlemiel. I don't know why — because I am from Wisconsin? because I am the biological son of a carpenter, the adopted son of a major league ball player? because I'm a guy? — but I want this guy, my fellow man, to nod at me at the end of the day, and maybe jab me in the shoulder, and say, "Know what? You're not like all the other limp-wrists I work for. You obviously know your way around a toolbox. Wanna go shoot some stick at the Twilite? Maybe throw a couple lines after some crappies this weekend then?"

But he won't. He won't, of course, because he probably doesn't drink, because he's probably Mormon, because LaEarl is, after all, named LaEarl, and he is of, from, in, and about Utah. He also won't because I do not exist for him. Not on a human scale, anyway. I am a job. I am the occasion for work. I am the thing he cannot do without but would ditch first if he could. His accent is semi-rural, and I bet he had to drive for more than an hour to get to my house. Moreover, I bet he had to drive to the warehouse and deal with a bunch of other guys like him who are all trying to get to wherever the hell the job is today because the sooner they get there, the sooner they can get home and change into their leisure jumpsuits. He is every bit of sixty years old. It's embarrassing.

"I wish I had some coffee to offer you," I say. We have no coffee-maker, never mind coffee. "I might run to the store for some. Can I get one for you?"

"That's all right," he says. "I appurciate ya."

I don't know that I have ever been told that I, myself — and not an act I have performed or a thing I have produced — have been appreciated. But Utahans are appreciators. They *live* to appreciate people. They absolutely would kill to be able to tell you how much they appreciate you. They appreciate the heck out of ya. It makes me feel a little unclean.

"I'm a milk man myself," LaEarl says. "The wife says it's my only failing."

I do not know what he means. I only pray he is not talking about breast milk.

"Yeah?" I try.

"Heck, yeah," he says. "Got a gallon of the whole stuff in the truck. Drank half of it on the way up here. Go through two, sometimes three a day when it's hot. Nothing like it for the joints, you know. Only downside's the phlegm. Everything costs something, though, don't it? Now let's see about those windows."

Clearly, there's nothing for me to add here.

He marches right up to the office window, takes a pass around the painted frame with a utility knife, and zip, it's open. He does not wait for my applause. He proceeds to open the rest before I can even unfold the little blade on my knife.

There is a metaphor in this, I know, but at the time he could have convinced me that he had super powers because he was from planet Utah and I, a degenerate coffee drinker, was not.

"Order says something about tearing out all the carpet?"

We're now in the dining room. The room is empty and smells like the garam masala doggie bag I once forgot in the trunk of Jenae's car for a couple of days.

I have already arranged with the carpet salesman for the installers (I imagined they would have been a team) to remove all the carpet so I wouldn't have to. I didn't know the first thing about how it was installed or how it was supposed to be removed or where I could take it if I could get it out of the house. But now I am alone with a sixty-year-old man who is asking me to give him an order, a command — something for him to do.

I want to tell him, Naw, LaEarl, I'll take care of it myself. I want him to think, This guy here is a good fella. I bet he could do this whole thing by hisself if he just had the right tools.

But I know he is thinking, Please, God, let this gosh-darned gentile (all non-Mormons are gentiles in Utah — even Jews) make up his mind so I can get my job done and go eat a corn dog and slam some more milk.

I tell him he had better go ahead and tear it out.

He takes a small, candy-cane-like pry bar from his rear pocket and with one smooth stoke rips the carpet up from the corner of the dining room and yanks it clear of the wall as though he's scalping the room.

As he pulls it away, I am amazed — not because there are indeed hardwood floors underneath the carpet, and not because the floors have stains of yellow and orange and brown, in fact all the subtle tonal variations of the urine/feces spectrum — I am amazed because I had never realized what carpet was. Just a topping.

The carpet is tacked with spiked wood strips that run along the walls, and as he yanks it up it sounds as if he is ripping flesh away from muscle. Once he gets hold of enough of it, he grips the corner of the carpet in both hands, squats down facing the wall, and springs up and spins around like a shot-putter, all in one motion. He pulls the corner up and over his head and marches the length of the room, tearing and ripping, dragging the carpet like a huge, stinky train from a most grisly wedding gown.

Before long, yards and yards of toxic carpet and disintegrating padding are draped over the porch railing like the skins of postapocalyptic beasts whose flesh reeks of naphtha and creosote. I wonder if asbestos was ever used in making carpets, because everything stinks now, and the air is chunky with particulate matter. I decide not to ask.

He is working like a machine, conserving energy by maintaining a steady pace. He doesn't stop or rest at all, and it's hard for me to know where I should or can be. Then he asks me if I want him to tear up all the tack strips that held the carpet down around the walls.

I wonder if he is going to be like this all day. Do you want me to take a break now? Do you want me to put the seat up before I pee? Do you want me to put the seat back down? It's kind of hard being an overseer, turns out.

"I mean," LaEarl says, "you might think about leaving it there.

You know, just in case things don't work out with the hardwoods and all."

I take what he says into consideration — he means the floor is certainly hardwood but it looks like absolute shit. But the carpet strips have to come up, even if we end up putting new carpet in these rooms. We've got to try. Still, I want to save him some work. At the same time, I don't want to be stuck with some huge project he'll need to bail me out of by the end of the day.

"Maybe you can just quick show me?" I say. And I notice that I am decidedly afraid of him, so everything I say tends femininely upward, as though I were asking him if my ass looks fat in this dress.

"Sure," he says. It comes out of his mouth like a curse. He cannot understand how I cannot understand how to pull up a freaking tack strip. In my universe, he would have just asked me where the space bar is and why it doesn't have a label.

He takes his small pry bar in one hand and slides the blade end under the tack strip and jacks it up in one swift motion. He repeats this five times, once per foot, and in about seven seconds the tack strip is up. Some nails are left behind because the strips had obviously been no stranger to moisture, but he doesn't fret over these. He flatters me by assuming at least this much inherent mechanical ability on my part.

"Get the picture?" he says.

"Yeah," I say, thereby acknowledging how ridiculous it was that I had, a moment ago, prevailed on him to give me such a lesson. But of course I don't have a pry bar and, until only a couple of minutes ago, didn't know that tack strips existed, never mind that you could reason with them.

He silently walks into the next room to finish tearing out the old carpet.

As I'm debating how I could possibly get the necessary tools, he drags the last of the old carpet onto the porch and I sneak into the living room to see what kind of surprises lay beneath the padding. I'm expecting more stains and bodily fluid Rorschach tests, but what I find is worse than that. It looks as if the floor is made of cardboard. Four-by-six sheets of white cardboard. Everywhere across the surface, the round heads of nails shimmer as though he has dropped a ten-pound bag of dimes.

"Masonite," LaEarl says. He is standing sympathetically behind me. He wipes his forehead with his hand, then wipes his hand on his groin. "My apologies," he says.

"What's Masonite?" I ask. "I've never worked with it."

"That's about to change right quick, ain't it," he says. "It's thin and strong and cheap — somewhere between fiberglass, cardboard, and linoleum. Once it's down, tends to stay that way. Great subfloor for carpet. You sure there's hardwoods underneath?"

I am obviously unsure about a lot at the moment. I ask him if he feels like prying up a bit of Masonite, since my pry bar is on retainer at another job.

He looks at me. He squints.

Once more, with a swift, sure motion, he works the blade of the pry bar under the Masonite and then hits the end of it with his palm, jamming the blade farther beneath. I expect a grand pop and release when he pulls the pry bar up — a hundred nails will fly into the air and a four-by-six-foot section of immaculate maple will be revealed because of the protective Masonite covering! LaEarl will make a couple of calls, and before Jenae gets off work we'll have the whole blessed Mormon Tabernacle Choir here singing a piercingly beautiful though tediously long song about how God saw our house through the trials of renters and crack cookery but lo! He hath delivered it — and these super-sexy hardwood floors! — from the hands of the wretched into the lap of the worthy!

LaEarl leaves the bar halfway jammed beneath the Masonite, stands up, and grabs the bar with two hands. He looks as if he's getting ready to lift the house, and I wonder what all the preparation is for. He's lifting with his back, not with his legs, and I want to tell him that he might strain something, but I'm too late.

He pulls up on the bar and instead of the whole sheet of Masonite coming up — instead of the great maple revelation I was hoping for — the Masonite simply rips around the tool, leaving a scar where the pry bar tore through. I can't see beneath the surface. LaEarl jams the bar beneath the Masonite again, this time a couple of inches to the right of the last attempt. He pulls up with the same result: a seven-inch tear in the surface. Finally he jams the bar between the two previous tries and manages to pull up enough of the Masonite to reveal what looks more like maple syrup than maple wood. Whereas the dining room just had a bunch of paint and shit stains on it, the living room floor is covered with some kind of thick shellac like that found on tables in northern Wisconsin taverns, or those toilet seats popular in the seventies made of Lucite with collectible coins floating inside.

"That's hardwood, all right," LaEarl says. "Wood the hard way might be more like it."

I nod. He's very pleased with himself for his partial entendre. I would be too were I not sure I could feel the floor beneath my feet turning into quicksand.

"Gonna be a lot of work for somebody," he says. He's smiling now. He knows it's not going to be him.

As he leaves to drag in the new carpet and padding, I am left alone in the still stifling hot room, which smells mortally bad. Masonite, about two hundred and fifty square feet of it, awaits. Masonite, I think. It sounds like an anagram for Assassinate, which is a thought, or Samsonite, which is luggage, which is what I feel like packing at the moment. Everywhere across the floor shine the heads of nails. A thousand shiny dimes. If only they were as easy to pick up. Think of all the calls for help I could make.

"You be all right for a while, LaEarl?" I ask, unwilling to look him in the face. "I'm going to run," I say. "Away," I leave out. I am willing myself — *forcing* myself — to finish the sentence and the sentiment. "To the store."

With that I hop on my scooter and set out like a latter-day knight. If Cervantes could see me now, I have no doubt he would favor not Quixote with his ass, but me — a thirty-year-old man driving an orange scooter onto the vast plain of a parking lot of a gargantuan hardware store in order to get tools with which I will wage war on a floor.

Fast Dancing

I TRY TO VISUALIZE what I'm told. Otherwise it's just words spilling from the phone, from somebody else, from some other place.

My mom, standing outside the door of Grandpa's condo in Waukesha. The recycling bin out for collection, blooming with Natural Light cans.

My mom knocked again. They were supposed to have dinner as usual. It was Monday. He didn't answer the door but she still had a key, so she let herself in to wait, thinking he must have run to the store for her diet tonic.

Just in case, she checked all the desperate places — the bathtub, the basement, the back steps — but he wasn't there. She made herself a vodka tonic and prayed silently for his safety. Then she realized: she hadn't checked the garage.

His car was there.

His car's there, she thought, but what's that mean?

It's parked on the left side, she noticed. It's parked on the left side of the garage, not in the middle as it always was after Gram stopped driving and they went down to one vehicle — probably, Mom thought, because someone else's car has been parked next to it. Probably because he didn't want the neighbors to see that that someone else's car came late and stayed too long and that he left in it.

My mother's detective work was slow and crazy, but it was not wrong. It was her. *Tonya*. And Tonya's blue Astrovan, with the brown passenger door from another vehicle. The same van that she used to park in the driveway when she came on Monday, Wednesday, and Friday to give Grandma a shower and change her clothes and her bedding.

An eighty-two-year-old widower with double cataracts, trifocals, and, likely as not, prostate cancer. With *her*.

"Guess where I am," my grandpa said. He was on the phone. He finally called my mom on Tuesday night after letting her sit and stew for over twenty-four hours. "He sounded pissy," she told me afterward. "Full of himself."

"Oh, for Christ's sake, Dad," she said. "Don't even tell me." She'd had several cocktails. It was just getting dark in Waukesha. The sun would be setting behind her own condo, and as she drank, standing up, leaning against the kitchen counter, the shadow of the sun would be filling up her backyard like an oil spill.

"Do not even tell me," she said.

"I'm at Caesar's," he said. "As in the Palace. You ought to get a kick out of this," he said, pausing for great effect. "We got married!"

"You did not, Dad," my mom said. She lifted her chin when she said this, like someone trying to get more air, another breath. Someone drowning. Someone being hanged. "Tell me you did not."

"So I can tell you're upset. That's fine. But I need you to take care of my cat. Just make sure she gets a whole can of that Fancy

Feast in the morning and then again at night. On a clean plate too, or she won't have anything to do with it."

"Tell me, Dad!" She was screaming now. It would soon be full dark in the yard and in the house. There was no moon. There were no crickets.

My mom called me as soon as she hung up on Grandpa. I was at work, and it was one A.M. by the time I got the message. "Call me back no matter what time you get home." It was her worse-than-usual voice, and considering what the usual had been, I knew this was going to be something.

We had only one swig of gin left in our apartment. Jenae heard the message and poured me the drink. I rolled a cigarette and sat on our front porch and left the light off.

"Well," Mom said, "he did it. He got married."

"To who?" I asked. That I had to ask that question was as amazing as the fact that I had to ask at all.

"Tonya," she said. Her name was like spit she couldn't get off her tongue. My mom was loaded at two A.M., Central Standard Time, even though she had to be up in four hours to walk Fairway, her morbidly obese cocker spaniel, and then go to work all day.

"I probably shouldn't have called," she said. Ever the Lutheran, my mom.

She told me the story. It took an hour and a half.

There was no comfort. There was no resolution. There was only the numbness and silence that the small hours of the morning held, still as a streetlight on pavement.

Once, my grandpa and I were in a terminal at Logan Airport in Boston. We were sitting on bench outside a *Cheers*-themed bar. I thought it was funny that they'd put a bar where everyone was supposed to know your name in a place where no one did. He was waiting for a flight back to his home in Illinois, I had just graduated from college, and the two of us had gone to Boston together to find an apartment for me.

He chose this time to tell me about his father, Charles F. Tucker. He did not go into detail. As quickly as he could, while we sat in the terminal as two strangers bound for separate destinations, he told me his father's story.

"He was a whoremonger," he said. I didn't know what that meant exactly, but I had a pretty good idea. "He was also an insurance salesman turned fraud and therefore a felon. He died in prison when I was at IU. He never met your grandmother." Grandpa took off his glasses as though to see if he still needed them and then put them back on. "And he was short. And his handshake was too strong."

That was it. This was my lineage.

Apparently Tonya had not connived to get Grandpa to go to Las Vegas without help. She had called him at one in the morning on Sunday to see if she could come over. He said sure. When she arrived, she had brought her twenty-four-year-old daughter, Daphne, and her daughter's friend. "Some Mexican," as my mom describes her. Together they got crocked and cajoled Grandpa into boarding a plane.

Grandpa bought them all tickets, paid for the room at Caesar's, and took them to a bar, where they drank and danced until four in the morning.

"All that fast dancing," he told my mom, "Lord God, it about did me in. I fell down three times on the way back to the room."

They were going to get married the next day, but he had called my mom that night and told her they were already married. For fun, presumably.

Grandpa told her how they went to the jewelry store in the hotel, but he shied away from Caesar's prices. They then went to a pawn shop where my grandpa bought Tonya a three-thousand-dollar ring, as well as some bangles and chains for her daughter, whose birthday was coming up.

"I know what you think of me, Patti," Grandpa said, "but I'm not a complete moron. I told her we had to sign a prenuptial deal. Well," he said, really enjoying the torture he was putting my mom through, "Tonya, Daphne, and her Mexican friend — all of them were stomping mad."

They soon acquiesced and made their way to the courthouse, since none of them had much use for churches or chapels. The last time Tonya or my grandpa had been in a church was for Gram's funeral.

"Daphne and the Mexican went back to Hogs and Heifers on the Strip," Grandpa said, "while Tonya and I waited in line at the courthouse. Tonya said she had to go to the bathroom, so I stayed in line, and it was moving along and I was getting worried and finally realized when I got to the clerk by myself that she wasn't coming back."

My mom was careful with the details, as though getting them wrong would allow it all to happen again — as though getting it right was its own kind of exorcism.

"She was back at that Hogs and Heifers," Grandpa said, "bunch of women's underthings stapled behind the bar. And 'I'm sorry,' Tonya tells me. She won't even look me in the eye. 'I love you but I can't marry you.'"

My grandfather was hung over. His hip ached from the previous night's falls. His knees felt brittle from all the fast dancing. He felt old. He had nothing to say except why.

"You know what she said then?" Grandpa said. "She said, 'I can't marry you because of my morals.'"

"What the hell did that mean?" my mom said. "Jesus Christ. Her morals."

The next day, my mom went to his condo and took down all the pictures of Gram. The day after that, she put them back up. The following day, none of us talked to the other.

We prayed it was over. Humiliation enough.

My mom asked Grandpa if he was coming over for dinner on Friday. The day after they returned. He said sure, that he'd love to. My mom thought it was all in the past.

But then on Friday he was late arriving and clearly addled by something more than gin.

"I'll have to leave a little early," Grandpa announced before he had taken off his coat. "Daphne, Tonya's daughter, wants to go dancing again. She says I've really got the moves."

"I am going to kill her," my mom told me after Grandpa left. "At the very least," she said, "I'm going to call her up and really let her have it. I'll tell her that the authorities have been contacted and that we have a lawyer. Oh, I'll give her a good piece of my mind."

"Yeah," I said. I waited for the rest of my words to rush into the pause, but they didn't come.

"And he's got his appointment tomorrow with the doctor," she said. "My God. What'll he think?"

I was afraid I knew. He'd probably think it was hilarious.

"I wish you'd write him a letter," she said, softening. "You'll know just what to say, Matthew. You're so good with . . . words."

But I wasn't. I didn't have a thing to say to him or anybody else.

All of this was so soon after my mom's own cancer scare and, of course, my grandmother's death. In another lifetime, I'd be able to see the sad humor, the tragicomedy of it all. That he'd spent his life married to a woman he loved poorly, one who wisely didn't accept his first offer, only to propose now to someone he barely knew, who would not take his hand either.

The next day, we waited for the results from his doctor. We knew it had to be bad news. We did not know how bad. We waited to hear, but we knew he might not tell us the truth. It was his truth, after all. But still, beyond it all, he's my grandfather. My grandpa. Gramps.

It seemed like only yesterday when they lived in their house on a bluff above the river, just off Route 9, in Mackinaw, Illinois. The light bursting from the west-facing picture window, my grandfather settled in his wing chair, his gray hair ablaze in the sunset. Deeper inside, my grandmother next to him in her low-backed recliner, the one Grandpa called her "boudoir chair," to which she'd say, "You'd know." Between them always a bowl of mixed nuts, golf magazines, an empty pewter ashtray, a mason jar of nail files, clippers, cuticle sticks, and dental floss. On a lamp stand next to my grandmother, a red plastic cup of oyster crackers. A crystal rocks glass of Scotch in her hand, glowing like amber.

A hundred feet below the bluff, the Mackinaw River dragging past. In between the treetops below, a canoe slides by. The smells shift with pending darkness. Citronella, scorched soil, fertilizer. Homegrown tomatoes. Fresh cut grass.

We have finished our game of golf. "Better to cheat than lose," Gram whispered, kicking my ball out from behind a shrub. Back at the house, golf is on the television but the sound is off. We are hot and unpleasant. It is high time to have another cocktail and be still and wait for the sun to set and take the yellowjackets and the mud daubers with it.

At dusk, Gram stands and flips on the track lights above with her wooden spoon. Raised a Hoosier and a Methodist, she believes in busy hands, so everything is made on the stovetop, and soon the air is jeweled with popping lard. I wipe the grease off the cookie tin so I can steal one more pecan sandy before dinner.

And then it is almost dark and the table is set and there is food on it and we eat. She has split a banana lengthwise, spread on mayonnaise, sprinkled it with Spanish peanuts, and set it on a bed of butter lettuce. This is our salad. The rest is fried chicken. Everything is as it should be.

We are all exhausted, but my mother talks, says, "Well, that *was* some kind of drive you hit back on eleven, Dad," and "You know, Matthew, if you'd only listen to Grandpa — slow, slow, *swing!* — I promise," and "Oh, Mom, this chicken!"

And then we are finished, and while it seems the birds of evening are begging me to shoot them, my grandfather is firm. "It is a man's job," he says, "to wash and dry the dishes." So he washes and I dry, and he tells me the story of how he was a hasty dishwasher in his college fraternity and a waiter once presented him with a dish he had just cleaned that still contained a scoop of ice cream.

And then it is dark in earnest, so we have after-dinner drinks — the same as the before-dinner drinks — and listen to the news — and then have a nightcap — and then watch the Letterman show, because we may be in Illinois, but all midwesterners are really from Indiana. My grandfather and mother are snoring in their chairs, and my grandmother feeds me her Scotch-soaked ice cubes and her oyster crackers, and *The Bridge on the River Kwai* is on TV, and though the sound is off, we can hear the soldiers whistling while they march, and I get her another Scotch and more oyster crackers, and a bowl of pralines and cream for myself, and in this manner we all will be forgiven.

But now. Now, I had to say *something*. I had to find just the right words. I'd get a good dictionary. Some heavy paper. A nice permanent ink. I'd write him a letter in fine, legible script. And I'd tell him. I'd ask him.

Dear Grandpa, it would say.

Love, Matt.

Lesser Acts of Transubstantiation

✳ ✳ ✳

AFTER LAEARL LEAVES, I am alone with the floor for a very long time. Stanley had nailed the Masonite in place with a twelve-penny nail every three inches or so. That's fifteen nails per square foot. At 300 square feet per room, that's almost 10,000 nails for the living and dining room alone. Each nail is three inches long, so I figure I pulled up about 30,000 inches — 2,500 feet — of steel. That's two Empire State Buildings stacked end on end.

Once I get the carpet out and the Masonite pulverized and then removed — which was itself a full day's work — we find waiting what promises to be the life work of a latter-day alchemist, because it will be just as easy to bring that maple floor back to life as it will to spin straw into gold. We know it's maple because Stanley had cut a sample out of the floor when he was putting in a new vent. The sample was a bright, glowing blond, textured with a gentle grain like a piece of driftwood smoothed down by sand and salt water. The wood beneath our feet, on the other hand, looks as if it had been worked over with feces and the remnants of a fast-food restaurant's grease trap. Moreover, half of the floor in the living room is maple and half is cement covered with one-by-sixes, then topped with tarpaper on what must once have been the porch.

And as if that isn't bad enough, there's a two-square-foot section where there might have been a fireplace or something — inexplicably, right in the middle of the room.

I suggest we create a little carpet nook where we can have a fluffy floor covering and big pillows and bean bags and such. The administration vetoes this straightaway. Having grown up during the home decorating depression of the seventies, Jenae wants her new house to avoid everything Nebraska celebrated: microwave ovens, wallpaper, decorative nooks, linoleum, wall-to-wall carpet. Our home is going to be bold and classy and it is goddamned going to have hardwood floors.

"Can't you just, you know, like, weave the wood," she says, "like this?" She spreads the fingers of each hand and laces her fingers together.

I explain what little I know about floors, namely that such a proposition would entail ripping up every floorboard on the end where it met the unfinished floor, removing or cutting back a sufficient length, sliding in new boards to fit, and then, finally, finishing the whole works with a sander and polyurethane and so forth.

"Not going to happen," I say.

She curls her lip. For the record, she does not say "Whatever."

"We could just carpet this one room," I say. I feel that's a totally reasonable proposition. "Think about it. We could have a supernice hardwood floor in the dining room and some, I don't know, casual elegance with a carpeted living room."

"Why not skip the painting too and just put the wood veneer back up everywhere?"

She's furious, and I can see discretion will have to reign here.

"Knotty pine then?"

No reaction.

It's a huge impasse. Our very first and, as with any respectable roadblock, potentially our last. Jenae is as opposed to carpet as she is to polygamy. Growing up with two brothers, she saw, I'm sure, her share of rug burns, but what she is so excited about in the bedrooms she is diametrically opposed to elsewhere.

We're like one of those oddly gendered couples on the Home and Garden Network. She's the visionary gay designer with all the big ideas, and I'm the sensible, straight, but dour girl sidekick who has to make a chandelier out of gum and broken pop bottles.

After a few minutes spent standing in the doorway, staring at the mutilated floor, she turns to me and puts a hand on my arm. "We'd be no better than Stanley if we put carpet back down on this floor." She squeezes and lets go. "We've got to save it, Matthew."

When I was a kid, I used to make up little quests. I loved the idea of proving myself, my worthiness — for what, I didn't know. I had a ten-pump pellet gun, and I would get all gussied up in camouflage, shoulder my gun, and ride off into the field behind my house. I had no idea what hunting really was, but at least I understood that it entailed shooting something. As the only son of a florist, killing things was never a family priority, so back then I would try to convince myself that if I got close enough to something and was ready, willing, and at least technically able to shoot, that would suffice.

Of course, the quest wasn't the same then as it is now with the flooring. I know my wife and the nature of the task at hand well enough to understand that coming close and not actually hitting the target isn't going to cut it.

It is nine o'clock on a Saturday morning, and I am sitting on a metal folding chair in a hardwood floor warehouse next to a woman whose too tight jeans, plunging neckline, and telltale scalloped lace bra hint that she's on her way to or from a divorce. To my right is a nearsighted bald man who keeps squinting like a subterranean accountant, and to his right are three handlebar-mustached men who appear to be related by more than facial hair. We are waiting for Tony, our teacher. He will teach us how to lay hardwood floors. But there are no Styrofoam cups of coffee. No camaraderie. No donuts anywhere.

We're all appropriately dressed in cotton duck or denim, which boasts of our readiness. I, of course, am an impostor in this crowd, but thus far nobody's asked to see any ID. The divorcée looks more at home here than I do (she just asked one of the handlebar guys to borrow his Leatherman and proceeded to pare her nails with its knife). The class is free and there were no posted prerequisites, though I can't help but worry that I'm going to be outed at any minute, escorted from the building, banned until I can prove I know a ball-peen from a claw hammer.

Therefore it is deeply depressing when Tony arrives. He is attired in khaki shorts, a pressed, somewhat silken golf shirt, and running shoes. We're hoping for this to be a mistake — maybe Tony's just a warm-up motivational speaker/comedian — but it is not. Tony is a professional. He does this for a living. He asks where the donuts are. Very funny, we tell him, Mister Professional Hardwood Floor Installer Guy. Very funny.

When I was an undergrad, the Very Reverend Father John Fitzgibbons Jr., S.J., taught a course on the American Renaissance that wended its way through Hawthorne and Cooper and ultimately found its destination in Melville, Emerson, and Thoreau. Father Fitzgibbons was a sweet, exuberant Jesuit who wore a baby-blue cardigan and a pastel-yellow knit tie rather than the cleric's black-and-whites. Instead of the minister he was, he looked like a mix of Tom Selleck and Mister Rogers. He was from back east and attended, as Emerson did, Harvard Divinity School. Though many of our classmates "read" those great American books with beery hangovers and an appetite for nothing more than the raunchy highlights involving underage Tahitian girls, gunplay, and/or impaled whales, as the semester went on, a few of us would stay after class like closet revolutionaries and continue our heated discussions. Before long, we proposed renting a van for spring break to make the thousand-mile pilgrimage from Milwaukee to Walden Pond with the good Father Fitz at the wheel. Though eventually most of us went in favor of the cocoa butter, cheap beer, and bikinis of South Padre — or just the Polish sausages of Wauwatosa — the impression of that spring was made for me in the margins of those furious books.

In the first chapter of *Walden,* Thoreau writes with open disdain on the subject of home improvement: "The twelve labors of Hercules were trifling in comparison with those which my neighbors have undertaken; for they were only twelve, and had an end; but I could never see that these men slew or captured any monster or finished any labor." The life of a homeowner is, it seems, one of perpetual labor and strife. But he also says in the same chapter, "Economy": "As is too common with writers, I got only my labor for my pains. However, in this case my pains were their own reward."

There is something essentially American about fixing up a house. Something perfectly democratic about doing it yourself. About not having a single damned idea whatsoever about the difference between a router and a planer but going right on and doing it anyway. Even if it means sitting in a warehouse on a Saturday morning in a ritual pageant of emasculation posing as a twelve-step program, we must edify ourselves and our homes. Thoreau, after all, didn't just go to the woods and live deliberately in the shrubbery. He built a house.

Thoreau brags in *Walden* that he built his shanty for $28.12½. Of that he spent $4.00 on "one thousand old brick" and $3.90 on nails. He spent more on nails than he did on windows. He spent ten cents more for his roof and siding combined than he did on nails. He and Stanley have a lot in common.

In class, Tony arranges a four-by-eight sheet of plywood that will be our "floor." As he readies his air compressor and nail guns, the handlebar mustache men needle him with tool talk.

"Those just brads you're loading there?" The middle Handlebar is kicked back in his chair, his fat arms crossed like two hams.

Tony loads a clip of nails like somebody who's watched far too many Clint Eastwood movies. "They're flooring nails," he says. He does not look at the Handlebars, but he knows they're there. They always are, I imagine.

The class is a total blur. Tony litters the floor with planks of hickory, and because none of us except the divorcée would volunteer, he hammers and nails the boards together quicker than he can narrate. He puts a board in place, taps it with a rubber mallet, and then *thwa-cock, thwa-cock, thwa-cock,* "and that's how you put the wood down," he says. His young son has shown up and sits in a chair to the right of the Handlebars looking grievously bored. He's clearly seen his father at his pedagogical best before.

Afterward, like all good "nontraditional" students, the divorcée, the accountant, and I vie for Tony's individual consultation time. This, of course, is what we had hoped for. I sketch my pine/maple floor for Tony as he coils the compressor hose. He glances at it and squints. "Not much of an artist, are you? Or is that accurate?"

"Yeah," I say, "I don't know."

"That section's all poked out there, right in the middle of the floor?"

I nod. "I just want something to stand on that won't make my wife hate me," I say.

"Good call," he says. "Then lay down your new floor on top of the old and let that tongue or whatever be. Put a threshold around it and I bet nobody'll even notice. If you can't fix it, frame it."

Whether that's a renovation truth or a cliché, I will soon find out.

In addition to whatever magic will come with laying a bunch of new floor, I also still have 750 square feet to strip, sand, and seal. The only thing I know to expect is dust. I go to the store to get the safety glasses and the face mask and gloves, and I figure I'm ready to roll. I just need the sander.

The rental department at Home Depot is not quite the gentle, welcoming place I hope for. It's tucked away behind the Contractors' Corner. The entrance is flanked with disturbing, improbable items with names like wet saw, rotary hammer, stump grinder — all of which, I think, would make for good stripper/drag queen names.

A man in an orange smock and a Grizzly Adams beard that begins just below his eyes asks what I want. "Glendon" is scrawled in black marker on the middle of his apron like a title or Scottish army rank. I tell him I want a drum sander. I rehearsed on the way over after having done a little research in *Home Improvement 1-2-3!* All the books I could find on the subject invoked the elementary nature of construction, as though reflooring your home or building an addition were as simple as counting a sloth's toes.

"No," Glendon says, "you're wrong." He takes a huge breath

through his nose that momentarily affects local weather patterns. "Drum sander. Jiminy Christmas. You do not want a drum sander."

I know he wants me to argue with him, to tell him that in fact I do know what I want, and it's called a Drum Sander. Either that or he wants to call me Sally and have me tell him his turkey pot pie is ready.

"I'm pretty sure I want a drum sander?" I say. With whipped cream and a cherry, I might as well have added.

"No," Glendon says. "No you don't."

He has his arms crossed high up on his chest, and when he unfurls them I flinch. He marches around me and walks back through the rental equipment. I don't know if I'm supposed to have a license to go back there or what, but he has already clearly demonstrated that he has no problem dictating what's good for me, so I stay put. He returns with what looks like a bright blue, cast-iron vacuum cleaner.

"Orbital sander," he says. "Works like a hand sander, only it weighs a hundred fifty pounds. Keep you from messing up your floor." He's entering information into the computer, not looking at me. "You can have a drum sander if you want, but you let that puppy get away from you for one second and you'll have a permanent wave in your floor deep as a doo-wop pompadour. That what you want?"

I tell Glendon that I'm sure the orbital sander will be fine. I resist the urge to kneel and kiss his ring finger.

At the house, with all my protective gear on, I'm as ready for an epic motorcycle trip through the Sahara as I am for a little sanding. The sander looks and feels like a cannon that's been converted into a Hoover, but it has a handle like a pogo stick. I wonder why until

I plug it in and give the trigger a squeeze. The whole contraption shimmies to life, shaking me like a scarecrow attached to one of those weight-loss belt vibrators.

I let go and step back to make sure I haven't electrocuted anything.

This jalopy is going to shake my bones out of joint, rag-dolling me behind it as I struggle just to keep my hands on it. The way all the books talk about running a drum sander makes it sound like trying to steer a drag car from the rear bumper. This was supposed to be as complicated as walking a schipperke.

But it's now or not-until-Grandpa-wants-to-pony-up-huge-cash time, so I squeeze the trigger and the sander powers up to its maximum orbital velocity of 3,500 rpm and I lower its big square head to the floor and then, instead of great sandy action, it just kind of shimmies there. A little to the left, a little to the right — no real drama. Lots of noise, but not much in the way of action. To get the thing to move at all I have to put my back into it and really heave. Even then it's like motivating an overloaded, geriatric pack animal. I pull back and find that, like vacuuming, the reverse stroke is much easier. But the prospect of vacuuming with a 150-pound former howitzer is not exactly something I was bargaining for.

I let the sander power down and slide it back, hoping to see a perfectly finished section of glowing maple. What I get instead is a square of subtly scratched wood. Whatever kind of sealant they used was apparently pretty tough stuff. It's time for a smoke break.

I sit on the stoop — on the same step I sat on when I saw the For Sale sign and waited for Stanley to show up — and I think about how every part of this whole homeowning proposition is shaping up like this floor. You think you can do anything — that you simply have to want to do something and all of a sudden you go from weekend warrior to master carpenter. You think you can fix something yourself and then, after countless hours of consulting books whose authors didn't imagine their readers could count past three, after spending thousands of dollars on tools you'll never successfully use even one time, after God knows how much wasted money on materials you measured once and cut twice — after all of it you still can't do it yourself. At this point there would be nothing more painful than telling my wife, my grandfather, some contractor — myself — that I'm in over my head. That I don't, didn't, and won't know how to swing a hammer and drive a nail. Vanity, arrogance, and misplaced thrift have cast me adrift in this unnavigable sea of construction.

Just then a happy little border collie trots up to my feet, its dad strolling right behind. We exchange hellos and he seems to want to keep walking, but I'm communing with his pooch.

"You buy this house?"

"Yep," I say. He doesn't even pretend to think I'm a contractor. "We bought this house."

"We looked at it," he says. He's probably a nice guy, I remind myself. My new neighbor. "Used to be a crack house, right? Been on sale forever. Two, three years, on and off."

I tell him I thought it just went up for sale, that it was only me and an interested . . . other person.

"This time around, maybe," he says. "He puts it up for months at a time, nothing happens, takes it off, waits a while, puts it back up. Anyway," he says, "good luck." He tugs at his collie, not wanting him to get too attached.

I go back at the sander with equal parts despair and vigor. I don't know how to process the fact that the house has sat unsold forever, but finding corroboration that the place was likely a crack house — it's liberating. I mean, when we bought it, it certainly could have used, as the realtors say, a little TLC, but we didn't know that it probably could have used a touch of TNT too. All of a sudden I feel that I can't go wrong. Or wrong*er,* anyway.

I rev up the sander, wipe the sweat and tears away, and I'm off. Pushing and pulling, a step and a half forward, a step backward. I try it again. A step and a half forward, a step backward. Feels okay. Methodical and directed, loud as hell and therefore kind of quiet too, inside all that noise.

I go at the room with the roughest-grit sandpaper first, trying to grind off the paint and filth with about a sixteenth of an inch of wood to boot. I have the windows and doors open, a fan going, but even so, I feel cocooned by heat. My goggles, face mask, ear plugs, and all the trembling, bone-shaking noise from the sander make me feel oddly protected, insulated. It's hot — really, really hot — but it's also soothing, pacifying, to be doing something that is simultaneously so much work and so much like doing nothing.

A step and a half forward. A step backward. It's like slow-motion fencing with a tremendously heavy foil, or performing the obscure mating ritual of an obese and mechanical race. After a few minutes I find a steady rhythm, which breaks only when I come upon a super-stubborn stain, and even then, I just alter my pattern to a step forward, a step backward, hovering for a while. From time to time I notice people passing by outside, and I sense their fear and pity, but I am impervious to it. I am in a womb of sound, sand, and heat. A step forward. A step backward. There is no progress. There is progress. There is an old floor. There is a new floor.

For the first time in a very, very long time, I feel at peace.

Time slows, liquefies, turns gelatinous. Something I can touch, poke, watch it shimmy and jiggle. A mandarin orange in a tub of

Jell-O. If I take off my mask, I think, I can breathe it in. Time. Space. Wood. I am grinding the floor into air, one sixteenth of an inch at a time. There's no reason I couldn't do the same to the whole house — pulverize it into dust, breathe it in. Through the friction between the sandpaper and the wood, I'm literally putting the house through a phase change. Solid to gas. For that matter, I'm sweating so profusely that I feel there's more of me seeping through my pores than is left inside. The floor, the house — it's in every breath. A drop of perspiration falls from my nose onto the floor and disappears into the raw wood as though it were dying of thirst for my sweat. I wonder how much of me it will take.

Suddenly I am torn from my reverie. Jenae's in the doorway, waving her hands, her mouth wide open — yelling, I presume.

I power down the sander and hear the tail end of her greeting. "Holy shit is that thing loud! I could hear it from two blocks away. It sounds like you're putting the house through a wood chipper."

She's wrong, of course. Only by degree.

The day proceeds much along those lines as I work through the first layer of horror in the dining room. I feel I've found a new monastic life at the handle of my new blue 150-pound vibrating friend.

But when I start on the living room, everything is much different.

First of all, the ventilation is meager at best, with only two small louvered windows and no way to work the fan without pointing it at the closed end of the room — I try once and a minor dust storm ensues. The next, more serious problem happens when I hit what I think is a particularly stubborn patch of paint or stain. The dirtiest part of the dining room had orange and brown stains outlining what once must have been a very large piece of furniture, or perhaps a holding pen for pygmy elephants, yet the sander tore right through them. In the living room, the floor looks better, but goopily finished. I think I'll be able to sand it right down, but instead it gums on the paper, balling up whatever finish is on the floor and then carving little spirals with the clots. I go through several ten-dollar sheets of sandpaper before I decide I had best suck it up and call for help.

"Linseed oil," Glendon says, before I have even finished describing my problem. "They sealed most every floor with linseed oil before World War II. That there is some crummy stuff—"

He stops abruptly, and I am sure that my floor-sanding nirvana is at an impasse. I know he's baiting me to beg for more help, but I'm deathly afraid that the only solution is to tear it up—that, or worse yet, he will tell me that it's poisonous and that we can either get rid of it or snuff it out with a bulletproof layer of Masonite and a couple thousand nails.

But he is feeling generous. "Get down here fast," he says. "I know you're still on the clock with the sander. I'll set you up with some stripper so you can get back to sanding by tomorrow."

What he gives me has more skulls and crossbones on it than advertising for a pirate convention. From what I can find out, it's more or less stabilized napalm. The warning on the label reads, essentially: IF YOU ARE PREGNANT, OR ARE TRYING TO GET PREGNANT, OR ARE YOURSELF A RESULT OF A PREGNANCY, BAD THINGS WILL HAPPEN, LIKE YOU WILL LOSE A LOT OF MONEY AND THEN DIE. IN THAT ORDER.

"So, any special instructions?" I ask.

"Seriously," he says, "your wife pregnant?"

I tell him no.

"Good," he says. "Take lots of breaks. Lots of fresh air. Stuff 'll mess you up."

"But it works?" I feel like a future war criminal or a Nazi doctor, about to commit some seriously grievous acts against nature and humanity — all for the sake of keeping our living room carpet-free.

"Bet your butt it works," he says. "Lickety-flipping-split."

Back at the house, I get geared up once more, keenly aware that I am walking a fine line between wasting a hundred bucks a day on a sander I can't use until the linseed oil is gone and destroying all the alveoli in my lungs and any other organic matter within a mile-wide radius. My detailed instructions from Glendon are to "slather it all over, then scrape it on up."

I do so gingerly at first, parceling out the stripper as though it's expensive mint jelly. I wait a couple of minutes, breathing though my mask like a twerpy Darth Vader. Then, with my little yellow plastic scraper, I go at it.

I feel a mixture of glee and horror. I have the power to save and restore things, but only if I am willing to sacrifice the environment and any present or future babies at the altar of home improvement. Then I realize it is costing me about five bucks a minute to come up with only a vaguely apt metaphor. For the rest of the afternoon I shake that napalm out faster than Westmoreland over the Batangan Peninsula.

The English word "pharmacy" comes from the Greek *pharmakon,* which means both medicine and poison. Likewise, the word "tool" is best defined as something that one uses as a tool. In other words, a hammer is not a tool if we don't use it as such. If we use a hammer as a paperweight, it's not a hammer. At the same time, if we use a paperweight in the shape of Liberace's head to drive a nail into a board, well, then that's a hammer. The more I work on this house, the more I realize that the world of home construction and renovation is chock-full of hypotheticals and syntactic subtleties. "Plumb," "level," and "straight," for instance, are all abstractions that rarely, if ever, exist in practice, no matter how often evoked in a handbook or blueprint. I came into this fixer-upper thinking that there were going to be categorically good or bad decisions to make, that home improvements would be markedly just so — improvements. What I'm finding is a nebulous world where trying to improve something means implicitly bringing it to the brink of its (or my own) destruction in order to give it a new life. I suppose this is true of everything. In order to perform most kinds of surgery, for example, it's necessary to anesthetize the patient and take him right to the door of death, press his face against it so his breath shows on the brass of the knocker, then drag him back for a few more years of shoveling snow and cheating on his taxes.

Thoreau said that we should beware of any occupation that demands a new suit and not a new wearer of clothes. What he meant, and what I'm learning, is that if you want to renovate a house — and if you want to renovate a life along with it — you've got to strip it bare before you build it back up. Any fool can take a sheet of linoleum or a roll of wallpaper and slap it over the existing surface, but before long the real thing is going to seethe to the surface.

I need to figure out, I realize, how to be a better man in order to make this house and our lives in it worthwhile.

While I work on the floor over the next couple of days, Jenae comes to the house straight from her job so that she can work on refinishing the kitchen cabinets. They are covered with, go figure, the same cheap wood veneer that's covering the walls, the refrigerator, and most of the appliances. Instead of nailing down the veneer, Stanley had apparently decided to save his nails for the Masonite floor fiasco, so he sprayed glue all over the original solid wood and stuck the paneling up. What ensues is not unlike my proceedings with the Masonite. Jenae would heave at a section of cabinet paneling with a scraper and all that would break off would be the parts that didn't have any adhesive underneath. On one cabinet, I swear I can read "Stanley" spelled out in glue and broken veneer. Occasionally I can hear her cries over my sanding.

At first I expect nothing but despair. Seeing her standing on the counter in her hiking boots, ripping at the nasty paneling with her fingernails, her hair sweaty and stuck all over her face, I think she'll fall and break an ankle, and then we'll be in the clear to have somebody come in, rip out the cabinets, and put up new ones, all in one day. For that, the average estimate we can find is $15,000 — just to nail some boxes to the freaking wall. But she sticks with it and does the same thing I did with the Masonite and linseed oil mess. She strips what she can by hand and then napalms the hell out of it. After that, she uses a hand sander to grind down the cabinets to the real wood. She stains them so that their original grain shows through better, and then she seals them and leaves the cabinet doors off: later, she'll sew curtains to cover the openings for a kind of café effect. I am in absolute awe.

I have never been so proud of anybody in my life.

The remainder of the floor work goes reasonably well, despite my expectations to the contrary. The sanding is slow and pensive, but as relaxing and enjoyable as anything that involves potential long-term hearing loss and nerve damage. It is as close as I'll ever get to meditating, I think, or to ballroom dance lessons with an automaton.

The polyurethane goes down easily and dries nicely to an only slightly wonky mirror finish. The floors that began as the arena for a shit-smearing contest come out looking like a suitable dance floor for a church. And the hardwood floor that I so dreaded having to add myself on top of the pine two-by-sixes — it is so easy and fun, it barely deserves mention. Tony's teaching served me well. The three-eighth-inch pieces of new maple snap together practically on their own. All I have to do is lay them out, fit them together, and nail them down.

Ridiculous as it sounds, Jenae was right: this house wanted to have a maple floor again. We didn't do anything but let it. For my money, that's what a good job is. It's not about forcing something to go where it doesn't belong, it's about figuring out what goes together and then not fucking it up.

We work and work all day long on the house, and when it gets dark we light every light and keep right on working till midnight. Dust and lumber and tools and stain are tumbled in every room, but from the outside, what a sight — what our new neighbors must see. The crack house that had recently had aluminum foil over the windows is alive with the sounds of industry, the brutal poetry of machines, and from its windows pour forth a kind of light made matter, glowing particularly with sawdust, sweat, and hope.

Remnants of an Ancient Sea

WHEN CONSIDERING OPTIONS for our kitchen floor, I think a nice tile or one of those cool industrial-style floors will be neat — the black-and-white floors you see in fifties-style diners. It'll be kind of retro chic, geometrically balanced, and relatively easy to clean. And if we don't get around to mopping every week, we can just move the dark dirt to the black squares and the light dirt to the white ones. Make a little game out of it even. Play dirt checkers, pet-hair chess. Also, I love black and white. Because I am more or less colorblind, things that have either no color or all the colors at once soothe me. I never feel quite so irritated as when people show me something that's a blend of a couple of relatively undifferentiated colors and ask me to tell them what I see. They show me a flower the color of a serious bruise and say, What color is it? No matter what I answer — blue, purple, violet, violence — they just laugh. No! they say. It's *indigo!* As though colors exist in a crayon box and have little cardboard fences between one another like solitary confinement cells.

Sadly, Jenae uses her executive veto on my diner floor. I think she's just afraid that I'll beat her at dirt checkers, but she won't argue.

"We are not putting any more freaking vinyl in this house," she says.

To emphasize her point, she pulls at the top layer of flooring in the corner of the kitchen. It is, I am told, a bright royal-blue-and-kelly-green plaid. Beneath it are what appear to be five or six former floors, all of which are at least as chromatically devastating.

"I don't see any classy black-and-white floors," I say.

"You can have your squares," Jenae says. "You may not, however, have your vinyl."

For the time being, I decide to forgo the battle for the war. I know, in fact, that I am going to lose, intentionally or otherwise, a series of small skirmishes before I can claim any major victories.

I don't mean to put this in overly martial terms — though, of course, the word "martial" is an anagram of "marital" — but I am definitely getting the impression that my opinions don't matter in the same way hers do. I am beginning to sense that when we bought the house, I got my study, the basement, and half of the garage, and she got, well, the rest, including, but not limited to, the bedroom, the bathroom, the dining room, the living room, the kitchen, the porch, the backyard, the front yard, and all of the side yard that you can see from the street. The rest of it is mine. That space behind the air conditioner — all mine.

I would never say it out loud to her, but I am beginning to feel that we are designing, remodeling, and inhabiting a scale-model dollhouse. Problem being, the scale is 1 to 1. And we are the models. The dolls.

"I'm thinking marble," she says. "For the countertop. In the kitchen. It would be so cool. Imagine how cool it would be. Literally. We could roll out pie dough *anywhere.*"

"True," I say. Marble sounds nifty, though I am pretty sure

there's a reason you see it only in ultra-high-end kitchens and in museums. "Seems like it's pretty rare in residential applications, no?"

"You don't have to be so negative all the time," she says. "Martha Stewart has it in her kitchen on her set. Why do you think that is?"

We are standing in our semi-remodeled kitchen. Seven layers of vinyl flooring beneath our feet. Matching avocado-green appliances huddle in the corners. Lovely new finish on the cabinets, thanks to Jenae's hard work, but everywhere else there is room for, shall we say, improvement. I can't imagine how we are going to use Martha Stewart as a role model when we first need a demolition expert.

"I don't know how fruitful it will be," I say carefully, "to set our expectations up against Martha Stewart's TV studio. It's not that I don't like Martha. I like Martha as much as any straight guy has any business liking Martha. It's just that there is a considerable gap between her corporation's budget and what we can try to chisel out of Grandpa."

Jenae crosses her arms and begins to quake. "Are you saying I'm trying to rip off your grandpa?" she says. "Just because I don't come from his money doesn't mean I'm trying to take it from you. You know this is your house too, and I was just trying to help make it a place we would enjoy living in and, if we ever sell it, see some of our investment back. I can't *believe* you. We may as well just rent again."

"Well," I say, "why don't we look into marble prices first. Then we can move back out."

This is a serious moment. Time for the Defcon 1 pet name.

"Muffin," I say, "please?"

Growling, then glaring. Then we kiss.

"Let me get my purse," she says, and with that, we're off to go rock shopping.

We pick the first flooring store we see. It's across the street from Home Depot, and compared to it, this little flooring place looks like one of those roadside sword-and-knife tents outside that Renaissance festival you never quite get to but always go by.

At the counter at the back of the store, a man and a woman are having a charged exchange. She's middle-aged and appears to enjoy attracting the attention of workingmen without having to try too hard to get it. She's sort of NASCAR cute, with tight but not trendy jeans and a tank top with an airbrushed wolf on it.

The guy has a stringy ponytail, like a roadie for a heavy-metal band, and wears surprisingly clean white coveralls.

Jenae's already miffed. We both hate poor customer service, but she especially hates it when it's due to flirting.

"This doesn't strike me as a marble kind of store," she says.

But before we can leave, the woman asks us what she can help with.

"Do you have any marble flooring?" Jenae asks. It is a dare.

The guy with the ponytail is still back at the counter, but his eyes haven't stopped considering what kind of help he needs from Miss NASCAR. His gaze moves from cheek to cheek of her butt as though he's judging a contest.

"Marble?" The woman glances around the stacks of cheap tile. We may as well have asked for tiles made from the teeth of infants. "For a *floor?*"

"Marble," Jenae says. "For a floor."

"Well, we don't have any," she says somewhat apologetically. "If you want my three cents, I'm not sure you want to put marble on a floor anyway. It's real soft, you know."

"Yes," Jenae says, "I know. For rock it's very soft."

"All righty," the woman says. She puts her hands on her hips and moves her elbows back and forth, a bit like a chicken. The air-brushed wolf wags between her boobs. "You want what you want. We don't have it. But I'm telling you, it's real soft. You spill a glass of wine or motor oil or something and you can forget it."

I say thank you and steer Jenae outside.

"Motor oil," Jenae says under her breath. "Like I would ever mishandle motor oil."

After a few more rodeos with recalcitrant clerks and would-be interior designers, we learn that marble is universally reviled as a residential floor. We decide against it, however, because it runs about twenty bucks a square foot. That's about nineteen-fifty more per foot than we have to spend. The alternatives we're left with are my diner-style checkerboard, the ubiquitous generic taupe ceramic tile we saw in every half-assed remodeled house, or slate.

My only previous experience with slate had been the blackboards in school. Because I had spent most of my time in cheap apartments or the houses of friends' parents, my flooring understanding began and ended with the unfortunate underfoot petroleum products: vinyl and carpet. With the chemical revolution of the fifties and sixties, everybody seemed to decide that it was better to fake it than make it. In other words, natural materials — wood, rock, cotton, wool — became passé. They were so *natural*. So timeless. You could go to a grand mansion in the British countryside, for example, and they'd have nothing but wood floors with old hand-loomed rugs — you could barely tell which century they were from, never mind which decade. But with the advent of extruded, spun, poured, and pounded-flat plastic, we created a generation of building materials that dated us almost to the minute. None being more fashionable than the flavor of the day; none being more unfashionable than yesterday's. New was it.

But real rock is back. The granites and the marbles are still by and large left to the countertop world, but slate is everywhere. It's cheap, about a dollar per square foot, easy to install (we're told), attractive, and, most important, it hides dirt well.

Once we decide on slate, the rest is easy, because now there are only two kinds readily available: really expensive and really cheap.

We place an order for the cheap stuff at a store that seems to cater more to professionals than amateurs, but we aren't shy about our ignorance, so the guy helping us doesn't hesitate to give us some pointers.

1. Pick the straightest line in the room
    to establish the floor.
2. Lay out all the tiles dry and then
    make all the cuts at once.
3. Hold on to the store's phone number,
    because they have a list of contractors
    who can finish what we mess up.

After the success with the hardwoods, I am newly of the mind that perhaps all construction jobs are merely tedious and time-consuming—not actually *hard*. The hint at how wrong I am comes in the form of a friendly offer from the clerk.

"When do you want to have the materials delivered?" he asks.

He looks as official a contractor as my hardwood flooring teacher. Golf shirt. Khakis. Imitation expensive pen. The kind of guy who gets paid because he knows how to get other people to do things that would make him dirty or sore.

"Can't we take it today in our car?" I say. I look like a poseur in my Carhartt pants, Red Wing work boots, and ironic/dead serious T-shirt that says, "This Dad Could Use a Beer." I look as if I might at least be able to handle picking up a couple of boxes of flooring. "I've got a truck if they won't fit in my wife's Beetle."

"Better be a really big truck," he says. "The gross weight is better than a couple thousand pounds."

We agree on the next day for delivery.

Slate — I had no idea — is mined. It comes from quarries in places like upstate New York, Vermont, China, and Wales. Part of what makes slate a superior material for both flooring and roofing is that it is readily split into thin, workable slabs, much like mica or other stratified minerals. Folks in the industry say that slate, especially, has "great cleavage." Half a billion years ago, what would become slate was a thick layer of mud at the bottom of whatever primordial ooze was around for Dick Cheney's first birthday party. It gradually became compressed into what we know as shale, and then seismic activity and tectonic compression formed it into mountains of slate. About halfway up Salt Lake City's Little Cottonwood Canyon is a sign at the base of a huge scree field that contains, among other rocks, slate. "Remnants of an Ancient Sea," reads the sign, perhaps a little too wistfully, but true. Pretty dramatic stuff for a place to put your feet.

Slate has been used for everything from cutting tools and weapons to headstones, driveways, blackboards and, of course, the eponymous little squares of rock that schoolkids used to write on. Though slate is roughly 4.5 billion years old, it's actually a soft rock, so it's a poor choice if what you want is permanence. Tombstones, for instance. Back in Colonial New England, slate was used because it was readily available and easily mined. But because slate has such an easy cleavage, if you will, time and weather rapidly efface whatever is writ upon it. Be it a child's primer, poetry, or an epitaph, slate has little interest in remembering whatever it is we have to say.

When the truck arrives with our materials, I immediately realize the depth of my folly. First of all, it is not merely a box truck, as I expected. It is a tractor-trailer equipped with a forklift. On the flatbed sits a huge lump of boxes, subflooring, and bags of thinset — a flexible, quick-drying mortar — all shrink-wrapped with BATT written on it in red grease marker. I expected a few boxes of tiles and a little stack of drywall-like backerboard — nothing more than would fill the back of my old Land Cruiser. The load on this semi would demolish my truck. There is nothing like the real-life fact of being crushed under a couple of thousand pounds of folly to make you wonder about the wisdom of doing it yourself.

Yanking up the old flooring is not the job I imagined. We begin pulling and tearing at the old vinyl only to find it glued to itself in the most onerous ways. A big sheet will come off with a tug, but then we spend forty-five minutes peeling away a particularly tedious section the size of a ham sandwich. All the books we have suggest it will be fairly easy work. Just take a flat-bladed hoe or a spreading shovel and scoop it on up.

While I am hacking one stubborn piece to smithereens with a box cutter, Jenae tells me to look up.

The light in the kitchen glitters with linoleum motes.

"Pretty," I say. "Wonder what makes it shimmy like that."

There is a pause. Even the linoleum stops shining for a second.

"There's no asbestos in this stuff, is there?" Jenae asks.

I say I don't want to know and just keep at it.

"Try not to breathe," Jenae says. "You know. More than is absolutely necessary."

Finally we get down to the subfloor: a layer of plywood on top of the joists. Because we're putting down the mass equivalent of a Nash Rambler in slate tiles, we need to gird things so we don't end up with a two-story basement kitchen. This is surprisingly quick work. Take a few four-by-eight sheets of three-quarter-inch plywood, and before you know it you've got a new, solid floor. Add to that a layer of backerboard — essentially a thin board of cement woven with fiberglass — and Bob Vila come smack my ass, you are ready to lay some tile.

In the space of a day, we have torn out an old floor — or seven — and put down two new layers of subflooring. We are doing it fast and we are doing it right (with the notable exception of having possibly contracted septum cancer via asbestos poisoning). Given the odds, however, I'd have bet against us long before now. It's not that I was hoping we would fail, it was simply that I had never known we could succeed because we knew we had to. It isn't about entitlement or vanity. We are doing our homework. We ask embarrassing questions. And we aren't afraid of the work. Nonetheless, given our friends' and families' recent track records, it seems like the perfect preface to disaster. But despite it all, we are pulling it off.

And then we rent the diamond-bladed masonry saw.

I am no longer feeling quite so jaunty. After all, you don't have to be a master of logic or physics to realize that that which can cut through rock can also happily make its way through bone.

The last time I rented heavy equipment like this, Glendon wouldn't allow me to get the sander I wanted. This time, when

I go to rent a piece of machinery that could cut a hole in a bank vault, he simply asks if I plan on using it for more than a couple of days.

"Save a bunch of money in the long run if you buy it outright," Glendon says.

I shake my head. I don't want this thing around for any longer than necessary.

"Don't put your hand under the blade when it's running," he says helpfully. "Or in the bucket of water when it's on."

"Bucket of water?"

All I see is a portable tray and a table saw.

"BYO bucket," he says. "For the water. Gotta keep the blade wet or it'll seize right up and, you know, fly off or something."

A blade that is tipped with diamonds. Has potential to fly off. I am taking careful notes. These are good things to know.

"Also, the pump thing?" he says. He picks up a black plastic square attached to a clear hose that runs to the saw and an electric cord to be plugged in. "It gets clogged easy. Use lots of fresh water."

"And the hand thing?" I have not forgotten his initial warning.

"Just common sense," he says. We're standing in front of the rental door of the store, next to a cannon-size chainsaw mounted on the back of a trailer.

"Common sense?" I say, as though it is a phrase I've heard before but can't remember what it referred to or how one employed it.

"Don't stick your hand in the bucket of water while you're operating the saw," he says. "You won't get electrocuted or nothing — it's got a good breaker built in — but it's hard to handle the slate if your hands are all wet."

"Common sense," I say. Not exactly what I had in mind.

✳ ✳ ✳

While I was picking up the saw, Jenae laid out the tiles. Our plan was to position them first, cut everything that needed to be cut, then slap them down, grout, seal, and call it a day. Ambitious, yes, but things have worked out well so far.

The slate, however, is in the garage. At the time it seemed like a good idea to put it there. It wasn't so much its weight as its expense. Don't want somebody running off with 2,500 pounds of slate, we thought. It didn't occur to us that it might be slightly inconvenient to get that same 2,500 pounds of rock from the garage, fifty feet across our backyard, up the back stairs, through the laundry room, and into the kitchen. The tile is packaged in what looks like pie boxes, though each box weighs 60 pounds.

Schlepping the boxes one at a time, Jenae looks prehistoric. A study of a female member of a Cro-Magnon, hunting and gathering tribe whose sad role it was to schlep.

"Need some help?" I say, trying to be chipper but not offensively so. If I am going to lose a hand tonight, I hope it will be an accident.

"How much does your vanity weigh?" Jenae says. She has just arrived from the long trek from the garage to the back door with a box of tile. "Mine's going at about sixty pounds a pop."

"Sounds about right," I say.

Glaring ensues.

The guy at the flooring store told us it was important to tap each tile with the handle of a screwdriver to make sure they were internally sound. If they were, the sound would be flat and firm, like knocking on a door. If not, it would sound hollow, and the slate would be good for making little slates, but not for flooring.

Jenae takes the lead role in deciding what goes where, since she is the one who not only can but actually does care about the color scheme. Before she gets even five tiles temporarily down, it is clear why people pay good money to have professionals do this.

The guy at the flooring store told us to pick the straightest line in the room. But now that we are in the room, trying to find the straightest line is proving difficult. Hell, trying to find any straight line is difficult. The ramifications are suddenly clear. If we pick the east wall as the guide, the line of tiles will meet the sink and the cabinets at an angle of ten or fifteen degrees. Whimsical, to be sure, but not what we are going for. If we start on the west wall, we will immediately run into trouble because there is only about one visible foot of wall — the rest is all cabinets, refrigerator, and sink. More or less straight, but not enough to measure by.

Fortunately for us, before we are able to do any irrevocable damage, our friends Erik and Nicole stop by for a little chemical and nutritional support. They feed us beer and pizza while we describe our stymied progress. Erik is, as Nicole rightly boasts, nice as Jesus but probably a better carpenter, so their visit is nothing short of a godsend.

Before he finished his degree in communications and became a professional photographer, Erik was a carpenter and general contractor. He and his uncles built a "cabin" in southern Utah that has four bedrooms, three bathrooms, a gourmet kitchen, a two-car garage, and floor-to-ceiling cathedral windows that overlook the red rock buttes. The first time they had us down there, Jenae and I packed sleeping bags and inflatable mattresses. The next time we went, we brought chanterelles, brie, and a '97 pinot.

"Yeah, screw the walls," Erik says. "Walls are never straight. Plus, you always put shit right up against them and you never see the floor there. Why have the main line at a joint?"

I nod and try to look thoughtful.

"Pick a perspective," he says, gesturing around the kitchen with a bottle of Red Stripe. "Like, where are you going to see the room from most often? Which view do you care about? You're not going to worry about it when you're in it. You don't look at a floor when you're standing on it. You look at it when you're walking toward it."

We pick a line from the living room and lay down a guide column of tiles that runs along the front of the sink. We build the rest of the floor around it, trying to remember which tile goes where by writing in grease pencil on their backs.

It isn't as though Erik is saying anything mind-blowing; nonetheless, it is revelatory. It's the kind of True Thing that you simply know from experience. I don't doubt that the guy at the flooring store would have given us the same advice, but there wasn't enough time to tell us everything we needed to know. After all, people do this for a living.

Knowing where you're going and how to work with the features of the rock are of paramount importance to any good installer of slate tile. Part of the reason why slate is so cheap is because it's only partially finished. The top of the tiles are more or less left as they came from the quarry. The sides are cut so they're uniform, and the bottom is milled so that its surface readily takes the thinset and dries without air pockets, which would cause it to crack or fail over time. In order to successfully install a slate floor — at least according to the charmingly perfectionist definition as enforced by the ministry of aesthetics — you have to not only lay the tiles out according to (1) the main line of sight that Erik told us about, and (2) the overall impression given the slight variation in color from tile to tile, but also (3) the unique surface texture of each tile. In other words, we were trying to orient the tiles geographically, chromatically, and topographically.

While I set up the tile saw and hold what I hoped would not be the last cigarette between my pre-diamond-bladed fingertips, Jenae lays out the entire kitchen floor. She washes each tile with a wet rag so she can better see and understand whatever lessons it has to teach, gauge its ability to fit in to the greater community of tiles already down, and then, after more consideration, either place it in accordance with her higher principles or toss it outside for me to practice my cuts.

I fill a bucket with water, set up the stand, gingerly place the saw on it, and prepare to plug the menace in. I know full well that folks with less supposed education than I operate these things successfully year in and year out and wind up with just as many toes, fingers, and noses as they start with, but I am not prepared to chalk anything up to a learning experience. There is something fierce, terrible, and holy about anything that can cut through stone.

I double-, triple- and — what the hell — sextuple-check everything to make sure I am not suddenly wearing lots of dangly jewelry, ponytails, or neckties that can get caught and wound up in the saw and reel my face into the blade like an about-to-be-spiral-cut ham. I don my shop-teacher safety glasses, hold my breath, and flip the switch. With an industrial scream, gritty water sprays my face like a shot from a horror movie montage. The saw is so loud I can't be sure that something hasn't already been severed. I turn it off and check all my fingers to make sure it really is water that's spraying all over. I don't know why I am so surprised. It's a wet saw. With that clarification made, I go about my ritual of enumeration, turn the saw back on, and proceed to transform a tile hewn from a multibillion-year-old rock into little Lincoln Logs of slate.

How like a child, how like a god.

✳ ✳ ✳

Finally it's time to lay some tile. I get a bag of the thinset, read the instructions, and whip up a batch to the consistency of cake frosting.

For a moment we kneel on the backerboard in prayer, the ancient tools of masons in our hands. I think about saying something to commemorate the occasion. Maybe we should write something sweet and sassy on the subfloor. After all, unless things go exponentially wrong, nobody will ever see it again. But we don't want to jinx things, so, without fanfare, Jenae dips her trowel in the bucket, back-butters some thinset on the first tile, slaps some on the floor, trowels it as if she's combing the wet hair of a monstrous child, and eases the tile into place.

"Good job, baby," I say. "You just rocked."

She looks at me and then regards the first tile suspiciously.

She lays the second tile in the same fashion, but it sits a good half inch higher than the first. There must be significantly more thinset under this one, but which amount is correct, there's no telling.

"Maybe it'll settle," I say. "Let's keep going and see what happens."

A flat, incredulous look from Jenae.

She butters up another tile, slaps more thinset on the floor, puts the tile down, and voilà! Now we have three different tiles at three different heights.

Jenae repeats the process with two more tiles, with similar results. The difference in height is never more than three-quarters of an inch, but that will be awkward to navigate in dress shoes, if not bare feet.

With what I would call indignant fury, Jenae claws up the five tiles and turns them on their back sides like so many hopeless turtles. The tiles in question have dramatically different amounts of thinset on them. The question is clear. The answer, not so much.

We decide to use more thinset on the floor and less on the tiles. We scoop as much as we can with the trowel, use its edge to comb the thinset into neat little rows, and set each tile back into place, jiggling them a bit and applying more force than I think we should. The result, however, is good. It looks as if everything is going to be just fine.

Driving back to the house the next morning, I fully expect any number of catastrophes to have taken place. We could have gotten the thinset consistency wrong and the tiles could have been buckled like the bed of a dried-up lake. Or we could have underestimated the specific gravity that comes with a slate floor. After all, we took away maybe 50 pounds of linoleum and added 2,500 pounds of rock. If anything went wrong, it was going to be not only costly but really obstinate.

There's something about buying a house that makes the world more permanent and worthwhile, but also more tenuous and fragile. You begin to fine-tune your sensibilities and notice more of what's going on around you because you are now a part of it. It's your neighborhood. Your yard. Your crack house, by damn. It's *important.*

You begin to make investments that renters and other, more transient folks don't. You pick up trash on the way to the dog park. You keep an eye on your neighbors' mail when they go out of town. You glare at cars driving too fast down your street — not because you have kids, but because your neighbors do, and that makes them the neighborhood's kids too. You stand a decent chance of inheriting them versus some random adoptive family if, you know, it came to that. You begin to see that just because something is the way it is doesn't mean it can't change.

The thing that I thought was going to be the most difficult about laying a slate floor — cutting the tiles — was in fact the easiest. After you lay all the full-size tiles, you put the tiles that need to be cut flush with the wall, mark them with a grease pencil, fire up the saw, and like Moses you have parted this remnant of an ancient sea — albeit with more help from Black and Decker than the God of Abraham. You have to concentrate when you're making these cuts, of course — no swatting mosquitoes, no playing with your pigtails — but so long as you take precautions, keep your shit together and out of the bucket or the path of the blade, it's as safe as anything. Just be mindful of the fact that you're dealing with materials that predate you by, give or take, half a billion years. Be respectful. Say please and thank you. Take nothing for granted. Remember that, as far as the rock is concerned, you don't matter much in the grand scheme of things. You probably won't even stick around long enough to make a very good fossil.

Getting Out of Sand Traps

IT IS THE DAY before Christmas Eve, and Gram is not here. Therefore, there will be no Christmas, my mom has decided. "We'll just get together," she says, "have some burgers." No one believes her. As soon as Jenae and I touch down in Wisconsin, we begin drinking competitively. And while there is no making up for drinking competitively with Gram, there is still drinking. I am not proud. Neither am I sorry. Everywhere we go there is an empty chair. You've never seen so many empty chairs.

We're in my mom and Bob's condo in Waukesha. It is too small. We all have to sit in the same room. The basement is Bob's "lair" and smells of Vienna Sausage and crème de menthe. It is single-digit cold outside. My mom and Bob are at work at the flower shop. Jenae and I sit with Fairway, mom's gaseous cocker spaniel, and Grandpa, who has threatened to bring Tonya to Christmas dinner. He said this to Mom, and she told it to me. If she could have, she would have canceled Christmas altogether.

Grandpa's prostrate treatment ran its course without any apparent hitches. At first, he was eager to tell me, his libido suffered tremendously, but — sadly — it has since rebounded and his escapades with women of varying stripes are back on. At the same time, he has since shown a new, vigorous indifference to my mom and to decorum in general. He has gone with Tonya to Las Vegas at least twice that we know of. She has quit her job as a nurse's aide. She convinced my grandfather to buy her a car (a Mitsubishi Eclipse — surprising, considering my grandfather would never have anything to do with foreign cars, other than the one midlife-crisis Porsche). He pays her some figure per month, we know not what. Tonya's daughter, Daphne, has meanwhile persuaded him to pay for her boob job. She also tried to talk him into buying her a new digital camera, but he told her she was pushing her luck.

So, we sit. David Leadbetter is on TV. His presence is invoked on the Golf Channel the way, say, Lincoln's is on the History Channel. Leadbetter is a famous golf instructor. As famous as they get, anyway. He wears a golf outfit with tight red slacks, a blousy knit shirt. A Panama hat with a floral print band. An alligator belt with a western-style buckle and silver tip. He is teaching us how to get out of a sand trap.

The Christmas tree has old-fashioned lights with little vials of red and green water that look like test tubes of blood and algae. As the light heats the vial, the liquid bubbles. It makes us drink and Fairway fart. We watch Leadbetter make it look easy, getting out of a trap.

Grandpa doesn't golf anymore, and neither do I. The last time we played together he had a transient ischemic attack, or TIA. A series of little strokes that, while not catastrophic, was not good either. I was visiting for a long weekend from Ohio, and we were playing a round at the club in Pekin. I had been playing a lot of golf then. It was the first time in my life that I felt I was getting good at something my family wanted me to be good at. I could drive well. I could get up and down in regulation. I could actually shape shots without slicing or hooking. I even broke eighty — playing with my grandfather, no less, and barely cheating.

We'd been playing a pretty good set of holes that day in Pekin. It was unbearably hot, as usual, and he hadn't been feeling that well—he kept stumbling after he swung and was slouching in the cart such that I was afraid he'd roll out if I wasn't careful. We decided we'd go in after nine holes, have hot dogs and martinis and call it a day. I was on the eighth tee, trying to keep my drive in bounds without ending up too short to set up a good approach, and the next thing I knew Grandpa was slumped down in the cart, slurring something about my shot.

I asked him what was wrong—did he want to go in? did he need a glass of water or a Coke or something?—but I couldn't understand what he was saying and he was getting angry.

Gram and I took him to the emergency room at Pekin Memorial, where he was the chief radiologist. We parked in his regular spot. The next thing I knew we were all in an examination room, and despite the fact that everybody was calling my grandpa Dr. Tucker, he was the one on the exam table, paper crinkling under his saggy bare butt, and he was crying. My grandmother held me tight; if she hadn't, I'm not sure I would have made it out of the hospital intact.

Today, the eve of Christmas Eve, nobody is crying. Despite the fact that we have a lot to cry about, we're all so mad at Grandpa that we can't even think about missing Gram. If he does, he has chosen an odd way to express it, by daring to bring Tonya to sit in Gram's old chair.

"You want to watch something else?" he asks, gesturing toward us with the remote control. There are two other remotes on the coffee table in front of us.

"This is fine," I say.

"What?" he says. His hearing has been deteriorating for years, which is fine with him. He doesn't like to listen to other people, and if it's TV he wants, he can crank the volume up as high as he pleases. If it's annoying to anyone else, they'd need semaphore or sign language to tell him about it. He futzes with the remote, trying to find the mute. He does this with both hands, as though it were a live bird.

I pick up the remote in front of me, mute the TV.

"This is fine," I say.

"Fine," he says.

Jenae is not good at this. She is good at talking when we need a distraction. She has a way of putting herself into the middle of a conversation and chatting until we all relax a bit or until we can't stand talking any longer — either way, she gets us together. But today, our first full day back as a family without Gram, and with only Jenae caught between Grandpa and me, such a foray would be suicidal, like windsurfing between Scylla and Charybdis.

"I'm sleepy," she says, yawning dramatically. "Can't believe how sleepy I am. Wake me up for the next happy hour."

She goes upstairs and I un-mute the TV.

Grandpa and me. We sit. Over and over again, Leadbetter gets out of the trap. The club head descends, slices well behind the ball — close-up now, slow motion — it looks like a blade passing beneath the sand, rippling the sand, creating a wave that lifts and carries and now propels the ball, up and up and over and out and then down the ball drops, bounces once, twice, three times, and then rolls gently toward the cup.

Grandpa grabs the remote again. He looks at it carefully. He reads every button, every time he picks it up. He holds it in his left hand and with the index finger of his right hand presses the power button.

It's the middle of the afternoon, we're alone, and drunk. There is a lot to talk about, but nothing I want to say.

"So," he says, but does not continue.

"Yeah?" I say.

He exhales as though the air he is forcing from his lungs is air I had just made him breathe.

"You seem pretty upset about something," he says. He is facing south, sitting deep in an overstuffed chair. I am on the couch, across the room, facing east. "You have something to say, I'd love to hear it."

I am drunk enough on a cache of Gram's Scotch that I should be able to say whatever I want, but I also know that I have never been drunk enough to forget regrettable things I've said, and I also know that my grandfather has never forgotten a single ill word anyone has ever spoken to him. It's not that I want to hurt him. It's not that I am scared of saying what I believe is true. And I'm not afraid of losing my inheritance or jeopardizing our special Golf Channel–watching relationship. The thing is that we're just about all that we have left, and I don't know what to say to make it any better. Right now, things feel as if they're getting worse, and he'll have to end up in a motorcycle accident or a bar stabbing in order to get out of his relationship with Tonya. It's killing my mom and I can't handle not being able to do anything about it.

"I guess," I say tentatively, "I just don't understand where you're headed in your relationship with Tonya."

"Oh, for Christ's sake," he says. "Is that what you're so uptight about?"

"Yeah," I say, "that's what I'm so uptight about. The fact that you're in some kind of sordid relationship with a woman who is clearly just after your money. You told me yourself that she wouldn't marry you because of her 'morals.' What the hell do you suppose that means? That she wouldn't marry you because you're Methodist or like musicals?"

"Don't be such a baby," he says. "What the hell difference does it make to you? So what if she's not a role model? We're just having fun. It's not like I've got anything else to live for."

I can feel my heart beating, pushing blood through every artery in my body. My blood feels too thick, gelatinous. I wonder if this is how he felt when he had his stroke.

"I thought you'd show a little more decorum in the wake of Gram's death. It's like you don't miss her at all and don't have any respect for the fact that Mom and I — especially mom, your *daughter* — are still mourning."

"Jesus Christ," he says. "You think everything has to be about how *you* feel? Like I don't get to mourn in my own way? Or that I don't get to move on, whether you're ready or not? Well, I'm sorry, but I'm fucking sick of it. I don't have forever to live. I'm sick of caring about all that shit."

I have heard my grandfather swear before, but not like somebody who might pistol-whip me. He is still folded up in his easy chair, but he sounds as though he's about to leap up and start hitting me with a length of pipe.

"Far be it from me to try to make you care," I say. "I'm just trying to tell you that you're basically killing your daughter and not doing me any good either."

"What the hell do you care? Who the fuck do you think you are?"

"I'm not supposed to care that you have replaced the lady who was your wife and mom's mom — my grandmother — with a not-so-glorified hooker?"

Despite the fact that I can't breathe or move, I find that I am crying. Much to my surprise, so is my grandfather.

"It's just that I love her so damned much," he says. He sobs, as I have only ever seen my mother sob. Heaving between breaths, his body unable to breathe regularly, unable to stop, unable to move forward. He sounds like a car stuck in deep snow, tires spinning, the engine hopelessly revving.

"I just love her too goddamned much," he says again.

I do not know if he is talking about Tonya or Gram.

Neither of us gets up. Neither of us moves toward the other.

Before long, David Leadbetter is back on. He is still in a sand trap. He makes it look as if it takes only willpower to get up and out.

Just when my family thought it had a lock on trauma, Jenae's grandfather died. Raymond, Lee's father, was in his nineties and had been in a nursing home for years, after a stroke left him debilitated and unable to tell the past from the present. Lee or Diane would visit Raymond daily in the nursing home. Every day Raymond would tell them the story of his morning and how he had spent it slopping feed or mending fence. In one sense, he was staying very busy. In another, he had left his body a long time before he actually died; his memories had taken over his body in a kind of revolt against the present. From then on, there would be no new memories. It was devastating to everybody but Raymond.

Jenae and I go to the funeral under odd circumstances. My adopted dad's son-in-law, Kevin, has just been named defensive coordinator of the Nebraska Cornhuskers. The Cornhuskers are to Nebraska what, say, the Catholic Church is to Italy. It was the only game in town and therefore a combination of your civic, cultural, and religious duty. The only way you could escape it was to flee. And even then, like a TB stamp on your passport, you're never really free.

As far as Lee is concerned, he has just discovered I am related, however tenuously, to a cardinal, a potential future pope. If I were related to the actual pope, it wouldn't have been nearly as significant to Lee as the fact that I am related via two marriages to the Cornhuskers' ruling elite. Suddenly it doesn't matter that I am not from Nebraska, not good with a pair of pliers, not handy around a shotgun.

We drive into the Republican River valley the day before the funeral and meet Lee and Diane for lunch at the café in Orleans, Jenae's hometown. It is a little diner that serves weak but scalding-hot coffee and chicken-fried everything. The mugs all have local business advertising on them, despite the fact that there are so few businesses everybody already knows them. Tripe TV and Carpet. Bose Transmissions. Mama's Salsa. Tripe Chevrolet. Bugby's Café. Nothing on the menu is over four dollars. Not even the steak.

The only people inside are farmers too old to work the fields anymore but too ornery to be put away in a nursing home. They all wear overalls, pearl-snap shirts, and mesh-backed seed caps. They all know Lee and Jenae.

"Boys," Lee says.

"Lee," they say. They shake Lee's hand and doff their hats at Jenae. They ignore me. They say how sorry they are about Raymond. "Awful shame to go that-a way," they say.

"Thanks," Lee says.

And then he can't help himself.

"I want you boys to meet Matthew Batt, my son-in-law here. He's the new defensive coordinator's brother."

Lee claps his hand on my shoulder and stands next to me as though we're waiting for our photo to be taken after defeating the last Democrat in the valley.

"By golly," they say. A couple take their hats off. Another couple turn all the way around to regard me.

"That's right," Lee says. He guides Jenae and me past the old boys to a table in the back where we can eat in peace.

"Well, I'll be," they say. "He don't look it, do he?"

Then, in February, my mom calls "with some news," she says. I am getting used to such calls, but also tired of them.

"I'm sorry to bother you, Matt," she says. Her voice is urgent, but significantly not sorrowful. "I know how busy you are," she says. "I just thought you should know that I'm at the hospital with Grandpa. Don't worry, he's all right, he's just, well, in the hospital."

I tell her to slow down, to tell me what happened. I have been reading Dante's *Inferno* and wish there were a tour guide like Virgil for the similarly strange descent we're making.

"We were supposed to have dinner together and I waited and waited for his call and I thought the sonofabitch went to Vegas again without telling me, but then I realized I couldn't be so sure. He had been having some trouble with his balance lately, no doubt due to the fact that he's smoking again and out all hours of the day and night for that matter with that slut and drinking vodka like it's going out of business — or what do they say, style? — that's it — like it's going out of style — because he supposedly can't sleep without it even though I told him to try milk and just warm it up in the microwave and he'll fall right to sleep like a baby and then I'm thinking maybe that's what happened, maybe he finally got a good night's sleep and is still sleeping and maybe it doesn't have anything at all to do with Tonya and so I decide I'm going to drive over there quick and make sure and his car is still there and the house is still locked up and I'm furious because it's exactly like before when he went to Vegas — the first time — can you believe we even have to keep track of *which* trip to Vegas?"

I quietly pour myself a drink.

"But," she continues, "it didn't feel like it did before when I let myself in with the key and I look around and check the bathroom and I hear him doing something but he's not in there and I hear him crying and my God is that something I never have to hear again, the sound of my own father crying, lying on his face beside his bed and I'm thinking that he was robbed or beat up or finally Tonya's ex-husband or one of her Mexican friends decided to teach him a lesson or beat some money out of him and I just didn't know what to do so I called 911 and tried to help him up because he was conscious but not responding like he should and then I realize, Jesus Christ, he had another stroke."

"Mom," I say. "Breathe."

"I know," she says. "The good news is I left his cell phone at his house and told the head nurse not to tell *anybody* except you and me where he is — that he is not to be disturbed under any circumstances, especially by anyone named Tonya."

She exhales, and it sounds as if someone has cut a hole in an inflatable mattress, letting the air slough out.

"I'm sorry I'm not with you right now, Mom," I say. It is not true. I do not want to be there. I am so, so tired of all the trauma. I don't know how people with big families do it. But, of course, they don't have to do it. They can just not answer the phone, because their big sister or little brother or great-aunt or second cousin will surely be there to pick up the slack. In my family, it is me, my mom, my grandpa. Thank God Jenae and Bob have stuck around as long as they have. We'd be practically nothing without them.

"Well," my mom says, "hopefully this will knock some sense into him."

I arrive in Milwaukee a few days later, after I tidy up my classes and prepare for what I hope will be a short and uneventful visit. The stroke was not a catastrophic one — it appears there will be no loss of speech, cognition, or musculature — but the doctors guess that he must have been lying on the floor in a contorted position for long enough to have done some temporary damage. They release him after a couple of days to a nursing home only a mile from my mom's flower shop for round-the-clock care, should he need it, and daily doses of physical therapy. Predictably, he is furious and my mom is thrilled. This means, for the first time in almost a year — since Gram died — there is somebody else to care for him.

I sneak a cigarette in the smokers' lounge at General Mitchell International before I go get my luggage. I know my mom is probably already waiting in the baggage claim area, and I know that this is going to be as hard or harder than anything I've done yet, so I don't intend to be at a chemical disadvantage. I try to concentrate on my breathing and muse over the fact that smokers' lounges are among the last public monuments to addiction, room-size metaphors of those syringe deposit boxes in public bathrooms. I contemplate telling my mom that I smoke. I've smoked for years, of course, but have never told her. When I visit, I wait till she and Bob go to bed or fall asleep in their chairs, or I invent short errands to run or start walking the dog four or five times a day. It's pathetic, I know.

The lounge is adjacent to the airport bar, and it takes everything I have to not go. The glass partition feels ridiculous: it only divides our chemical wants and needs from each other momentarily.

My grandfather was/is also a closet smoker. He used to take the trash out several times a day. As a kid, I never understood why my grandparents never got a bigger trash can. Even in their kitchen they had this little one-gallon deal.

"Why don't I get that, Gramps?" I'd say, going for the trash.

"No, no, no," he'd say, practically shoving me back down onto the couch. "Just take me a second and I forgot my billfold in my car anyway."

"Didn't you just get your wallet a minute ago?"

"I meant my checkbook," he'd say, and then be gone for five minutes and come back smelling like a campfire.

I didn't get it even when I actually saw the cigarette butts in his car. The ashtray was always overflowing with butts, and there were burn marks in the seats, the console, even the fabric on the ceiling, yet I never understood that he smoked.

Of course I knew on some level, but I never caught him at it, and so therefore he did not smoke. But finally, I realize, he is living a life that neither my mother nor I can ignore, no matter how badly we want to. First with Tonya, now with his stroke.

I snub out my cigarette, fish around in my carry-on for a handful of Altoids, and hop on the escalator, descending into I know not what.

My suitcase is already there, and I grab it from the carousel and go to the usual spot at the beginning of the pick-up loop to look for my mom. If there had been a way to turn around and get back on the same plane I had just left without committing a federal crime, I would have. I feel small and puerile. I don't know whether I can handle this right now. It is ostensibly my last semester of course-work at the university, and I have to get a committee together for my defense and prepare for my exams and start thinking about a dissertation and all that crap, and then this — *life* — all the while.

I hear a little beep, and around comes my mom in her minivan, the FLRLDY license plate smiling ahead.

Before I know it she pops out and shouts, "Hi, turkey leg!" She gives me a big hug and kiss and tells me I look great. It is about four degrees Fahrenheit and the wind is blowing in off Lake Michigan, making it feel dangerously colder. "Grandpa's with me," she says. She gestures toward a quilt-swaddled figure in the back seat. "We have to take him back, but he really wanted to come." She holds my face in her hands. "I'm so glad you're here," she says. "What a treat!"

Before I put my bags in the back, I check the license plate to make sure I'm getting into the right vehicle. She seems perky and chipper — more so than she ever was over Christmas or, for that matter, any time over the past year.

Grandpa opens his door and teeters out. He is wearing a bathrobe underneath the extra-large topcoat I gave him for Christmas. I actually bought the coat for myself at, of all places, a J. Peterman sale a while back. It was what they used to call a greatcoat. It was the kind of coat a father would pass down to his son. I loved the coat so much I considered gaining weight just to fit into it. It is jarring, to say the least, to find my grandfather, dressed otherwise like a hospital patient, infirm and trembling from cold and atrophy, wearing my greatcoat.

"Hi, Grandpa," I say.

He starts crying.

I am worried that this will be the beginning of another devastating trip, but my mom is humming "On the Street Where You Live" from *My Fair Lady,* and off we go for some cocoa and then to tuck Grandpa into bed.

I only stay through the weekend, because I have to, and can, leave. I have the nicest visit with my mom, because for the first time in a very long time we don't have to cater to Grandpa's mercurial tempers or earsplitting TV volumes. We pick him up at lunch and take him to Culver's for butterburgers, onion rings, and a little frozen custard, and then back to the nursing home he goes. It isn't exactly fun, but it isn't anywhere near as bad as it had been a month ago at Christmas. By the time we get home it's nighttime, so I cook up some pork chops and mashed potatoes for Mom and Bob, and because I use half a stick of butter per person, Bob is happy as can be. He's in bed by eight, as is his wont, and then my mom and I sit up and drink gimlets and watch Meg Ryan movies (except the freaky one where she's an abusive alcoholic — a little too close to home) and talk about how it wasn't supposed to be like this, but it is, and we're just dealing with it as best we can. We cue up *When Harry Met Sally,* back to that funny fight about the wagon wheel coffee table.

They figure that Grandpa will be able to live on his own again before too long, though he will have to endure months of physical therapy.

My mom and I have mixed feelings. Of course we don't want him to be sick or to suffer. But neither do we want him tearing it up again in Las Vegas or cavorting around greater Milwaukee with his charm school dropouts. The facts remain: he is too old to behave like this; he is legally blind in one eye and can't see well enough to drive; he is burning through his retirement money quicker than if he literally set it on fire; he dreads our company but can't stand to be alone when he isn't with Tonya.

Then in April, when he's nearly back to full strength, and on the one-year anniversary of Gram's death, comes the big solution: Grandpa is going to move in with my mom and Bob.

Grandpa thinks it is his master plan that's going to solve all the problems. He will cut his expenses in half and probably do the same for Mom and Bob. He'll pay rent, and chip in for groceries and utilities and so forth, and thereby everybody will save money. Grandpa won't be tempted to see Tonya anymore because there's no way Tonya is coming to my mom's house, leaving her sooty butt prints everywhere. To boot, they'll probably make a killing by selling all his furniture and whatnot from the condo.

The only thing Grandpa overlooked was the fact that he hates Bob, and Bob hates him back. Nothing more than a civil "Robert," "Robert" exchange has passed between them in years. What could be a better idea than to put them under the same roof in a two-bedroom condo? On top of that, Fairway and Grandpa's cat are both so old and recalcitrant that there's no way those two can live together in any state but, well, like dogs and cats.

But it never comes to that. Shortly after Grandpa begins packing, his cat goes missing. The next morning, a neighbor finds her on Racine Avenue, directly behind Grandpa's condo, dead in the middle of the road. A good portent it does not make.

In Defense of Dilettantes

ONE WAY I DO NOT like to wake up is to my dog barking her *Emergency! Intruder! Alert!* bark. Maggie does not bark this bark often, as is her meek spaniel way, but when she does it's usually because I have overslept and someone is knocking at the door. That someone, of course, might have been scheduled to arrive, but he might have shown up early. Today that not-so-hypothetical someone is Steve, a kind of construction renaissance man whose latest medium happens to be cement. He's pouring our concrete countertop this morning, and apparently that means a good time to Steve. So good a time that he shows up nearly an hour earlier than we arranged, on Presidents' Day, the best Monday of the year to sleep in for students, teachers, bankers, federal employees — everyone.

Aside from rousing me from a weird dream about my grandfather, an ice cream truck, and a jazz concert featuring Julian "Cannonball" Adderley and me, what Steve has done is bring to light the fact that no matter what I pretend to know after six months of home improvementing, I'm still every bit a dilettante. He's disgusted, I can tell, that I am not already awake at nine o'clock, that I have started my week thusly, that I made him wait outside a locked door like a common peddler or a missionary.

"Oh, hey, I didn't hear you — "

"Surprise," he says and pushes past me with a bucket of tools.

My friend Bryan used to call me a dilettante whenever I ran out of tobacco. We both rolled our own Gauloises (if we couldn't be French or Frank O'Hara, at least we could smoke like them), but Bryan was a professional and always had plenty of papers and tobacco, his Zippo gassed up and ready to go. I've smoked for a few years, basically aligned with my tenure as a grad student, and I've never smoked more than a dozen cigarettes a day. Lately I've settled down to three or four. Mostly I'm in it for the accoutrements. Bryan's right: I am ever the dilettante. If he only knew how long it takes me to make one small cut with a Skil saw.

On the home improvement front — or should I say the manhood front, because being able to work on and maintain your home has, as far as conventional wisdom goes, everything to do with being a man — today Steve continues to delineate the field.

Real men rise early and have big breakfasts that involve cast-iron skillets, sausage cut from a tube, and as many cracked eggs as you can coerce from the henhouse. You don't wear work clothes unless they're worn and threadbare at the knees and thighs, but still look new around the butt, because if they're worn there, they have been mostly sat in. You drive cars that are somehow inappropriate to their job. They're either too small — like Steve's Reagan-era Subaru, on which he straps everything, including a sandwich of four-by-eight sheets of plywood, some two-by-fours, and a bunch of angle irons — or they're grotesquely 'roided-up four-by-four pickups with sixty-inch lift kits and glasspack exhaust systems that can disintegrate kidney stones. You never admit to needing help. You "might could use a hand" every now and then, but only in an if-you're-just-gonna-sit-there-and-be-an-embarrassment kind of way. You never have anybody do for you what you should be able to do for yourself. That's about as golden a rule as it gets in this testosterone-addled field. Do it yourself, motherfucker. I can hear Bryan now, cigarette in hand, waiting to be licked finished. What's the matter? *Pussy hurt?*

A few jobs, however, are not worth doing. Jobs treated with almost universal disdain even in the hallowed Halls of Balls. Sheetrocking, for instance. Stripping paint. Insulating. All such jobs are levied to the recently paroled, habitually recidivist, newly immigrated, or woefully undocumented. They're uniquely back-breaking, nut-busting tasks that require a very specific skill set, but not much in the way of organizational wherewithal or industry credentials. The type of work men pass on as soon as they can. I mean, you could do it if you had to, but there's a kind of glory in being able to put some jobs beneath you. Besides, how many times does a guy really need his intestines to pop through his abdomenal wall?

And it's not all about money. To subcontract drywallers, for example, is expensive. But the difference between that and, say, laying your own plumbing is that there's pride and distinction to be had in exemplary plumbing. I mean, instant, plentiful hot water. Clear drains. Drip-free faucets. Rapidly vacating flushes. It's inconspicuously miraculous work. You've done that which had been unimaginable for all but the last few ticks of human history. You've diverted the river, tamed it, ushered it right into the house without washing the foundation away. The plumber, after all — not the physician or the politician — is responsible for the rise of civilization.

Put that up against drywalling. It doesn't matter that hanging a good wall requires perhaps as much in the way of skill and artistry as making a mosaic. It doesn't matter that drywalling demands patience and devotion approaching orthodoxy. A good team of drywallers can rough-in a house in an afternoon, but to turn a bunch of sheets of raw material screwed to two-by-fours into smooth, right-angled, crisp-cornered walls takes days of taping, mudding, plastering, and sanding, none of which can be done on the same day because each layer needs its own time to dry. It's so intensive and tedious you'd never think drywall is the descendant of the clay and wattle of the mud hut. Sadly, to most people none of that matters. Just about any wall is a good wall unless it has a hole in it, never mind that it took the better part of a hundred man-hours to get it right. If Jesus were alive today, I don't think he'd be a carpenter. Carpentry is too glamorous for the only son of the Lord. Jesus, he'd be a drywaller.

Incidentally, Michael, our old archangel neighbor, is a plasterer — essentially the Old Testament version of a drywaller. Though little new construction calls for plaster walls, there are lots to patch and repair, including ours. When Michael stopped by one day to check the place out, I asked him what he thought I should do to repair the wall where Stanley had glued yards of faux paneling. When we took it off, chunks of the old plaster came with it, and the only thing I could think to do was to get new paneling.

"That hose work out front?" Michael asked. In under five minutes he whipped up a batch of plaster and spread it on the wall smoother than frosting on a wedding cake. It was perfect. It was a new wall. It was miraculous.

"You're a healer, Michael," I said. "I can't believe it. What do I owe you?"

Michael quietly scraped off his trowel. "Hey, it's what I do. Call it a housewarming present."

He was an artist and a saint.

✳ ✳ ✳

Now, installing a kitchen countertop is not a job you want left to just anyone. A countertop is one of those household jewels that people use as a selling point. Frank Lloyd Wright design. Wooded lot. Radiant-heat floors. *Fill-in-the-blank* countertop. As though any of those things couldn't occur in a double-wide just as easily as in an estate home. But of course we buy and sell via synecdoche. You can't advertise the whole house (. . . you'll notice the lovely slate kitchen floor, which was fabricated using primarily Indian and Chinese slate, laid atop properly spaced old-growth quarter-sawn oak joists on Georgia-harvested three-quarter-inch pine pulp plywood, half-inch backerboard made with pride by the men and women of Hickory, North by-God Carolina . . .). You just can't tell it all, so you push the finer points. Connect the dots. As in Joyce's *Dubliners* story "Araby," where we get Mangan's sister with a swinging dress and a soft rope of hair, and instead of fearing her a victim of hanging, we are as smitten as eight-year-old seminary students. Same thing with real estate, where we take "stainless steel," "skylights," and "vaulted ceilings" and think not of a Scranton rivet factory but a Scarsdale country mansion.

But just because countertops are focal selling points of a house, they don't necessarily equal a do-it-yourself project. After all, we're talking about beaucoup de work here. And if you mess this up, well, your wife will ever be reminded of the pathetic little bedwetter she married instead of the Harley-throttling stud she should have, because the evidence is right there in the middle of your kitchen. It's the first thing guests see in the room; it's where you put down your car keys and your grocery bags; it's where you chop your broccoli and pour your wine and scramble your eggs; and when you have a party, it's where everyone puts down their Harvey Wallbangers and absent-mindedly caresses the smooth, hard, cold surface. Nowhere else does your house get such concentrated tactile attention. It had damned well better be good.

We were hoping to do as much work on the house ourselves as possible, but there was some stuff we couldn't or wouldn't do. To help assuage my self-imposed guilt, I convinced myself that the best countertops are solid stone or manufactured materials. That is, they're one big freaking piece fabricated in a quarry in Brazil or a factory in Taipei. Where's a workingman supposed to fit himself in?

Countertops are like poetry according to Yeats: if you can see evidence of the work, all the stitching and unstitching is for naught. A countertop shouldn't look like it was the first one you made and installed. There's no room for a learning curve here. Countertops are supposed to appear as though they were created just for your kitchen — as though no other place in the world could possibly have the same one. Countertops must not, however, show any evidence of manufacture. A countertop must simply *be.* If a craftsman wants attention, he can build the cabinets that stand above. He can router the maple doors or craft glass panes with images of dainty fairies whispering each to each, but the countertop itself will never garner any accolades for your labors. Unless you're Steve.

Driving down to meet Steve in his house in Orem, Utah, we had no idea what to expect. All we knew of Steve was that Jenae's friend's husband, Mattson, knew him growing up. Shortly after Steve had built his first countertop — his own — he did Mattson's mom's. Mattson thought he had probably done a couple more. It felt as if we were investing in some sketchy venture that might involve ritual scarification. He lived in Orem, after all. If Provo is the Vatican City of the Mormon culture, then Orem would be whatever Italian city lies outside those holy gates. Except that city is probably something lovely and, at the very least, Italian. This city is Orem. Like Oreo but with an *m,* and not so sweet or racially diverse as the cookie. All I wanted to know about Orem I learned from their billboards for "Hot LDS Singles," a Mormon movie called *The Singles Ward* about cheery but awkward virgins, and a Mr. Mac suit store that outfits "more missionaries than anyone!" It's also the city that Gary Gilmore made infamous via a double murder — the story behind Norman Mailer's book *The Executioner's Song. That* they don't have on a billboard.

Inside Steve's house we found our Orem doppelgänger. The outside looked as boxy and modest as a cigar cutter's hut, but inside everything was bright and warm, light and cool, with muted colors and clever antiques. It was like going from some drab abscess of a night into a cheery pottery gallery with mulled cider and fresh sugar cookies. It didn't hurt that his wife had in fact just made mulled cider and sugar cookies. They had refinished hardwood floors, earthy tile in their kitchen, colors that reminded me of a child's sock drawer, and salvaged, galvanized grain bins serving as coffee tables, replete with tumbled-glass bottles that looked as though they'd delivered a hundred desert-island epistles each.

Also, they had no TV. It made the room oddly, though comfortably, square. Whereas in most American homes, including ours, living rooms are three-walled theaters with all attention drawn toward the pretty blue talking box, Steve's felt like a place where, at any minute, we could have one of those "conversations." But as tends to come with the TV-free of our breed, I also sensed a slight air of superiority. Not in a pompous, lording way. Not even in an aggro Kill Your Television bumper sticker way. It was an understated, modest superiority. His home lacked what anchored every room in the house I grew up in. In my mom's condo, for example, there's nary a spot where you can escape the stare of a TV — not even the bathroom. If all her TVs were cameras, it'd be supermax-prison secure. Steve's house was little, quaint, cheery, homey, and unplugged.

Steve, I was learning, is the kind of guy who wears the same Carhartt pants, threadbare T-shirt, and hiking boots everywhere he goes. That singular an identity, that comfortable a home, all that confident simplicity . . . I didn't merely look up to him; I wanted to *be* him. At the very least, I wanted him to make our countertop.

Every decision he had made in his life seemed to have a deliberate, thoughtful, independent feel to it. The countertop in his house was the only one we had to see, though I doubt we actually had to see it. It was Steve we wanted. Hiring Steve was the opposite of picking up some subcontractor/hooker from Home Depot. It was an antidote to the thugs who wore their tool belts like varsity jackets and stuffed logs of soppressata down their pants. It was as though he was a friend of ours. Or someone we wished was our friend. Someone who undoubtedly was good at playing chess, identifying and naming conifers, making unusual but irresistible shish kebobs. Never mind that the countertop in his house looked like hardened chocolate pudding. Never mind that his rates were the same as a licensed concrete countertop company in Ogden. Never mind that Steve had probably been to one of Mattson's disturbing parties, which purportedly feature naked people somehow sliming around inside a forty-gallon drum with the aid of a huge sheet of Mylar and five or six quarts of Wesson oil. Never mind all of that. Steve was, at least for the time being, who we wanted.

A bonus to the whole proposal was that Steve was something of a dilettante himself. While he never actually said how many countertops he'd made, he kept mentioning the same two over and over again: his, the first, and Mattson's mom's, the second. In some obvious ways that made him a liability, but in others it made him an asset. For one thing, we were paying by the square foot, not by the hour.

The best part for me was that he was going to let me help him. I don't know if "let me" is exactly the way to put it. After all, the existing countertop was a hundred-pound pain in the ass, the approximate size and portability of an L from the HOLLYWOOD sign. I'm sure he could have managed it on his own, but I don't think he would have liked it.

My biological father, on the other hand — a carpenter in Alaska — once told someone he charged twenty-five dollars an hour to do a job alone, fifty if the homeowner wanted to watch. And if the guy wanted to help, the rate was one hundred bucks an hour.

From the beginning, Jenae and I wanted unique stuff, but I wanted unique-on-the-cheap and she wanted, well, boutique-unique. The kitchen, in particular, had at one time included plans for a ten-thousand-dollar commercial Wolf range that could roast a flock of Cornish hens, an eight-thousand-dollar, artificially intelligent Sub-Zero refrigerator, a fifty-dollar-per-square-foot hand-harvested Indian slate floor, a Creamsicle-colored Italian marble countertop, two five-hundred-dollar steampunk ceiling fans, and three-hundred-dollar-apiece schoolhouse pendant lights that we would fit with hand-blown lightbulbs made by (based on the price) Edison himself. By and large, the issue of financing the dream kitchen made my case the more viable one, but hers remained the compass for our design.

While the compromises we made in scratch-and-dent appliances and cheap-but-still-exotic slate floors were invisible to everyone but us, the countertop could not look as if we got a deal on it. To a certain way of thinking, it would be like asking your dearly beloved to marry you and then putting a ring on her finger crafted out of a Hamm's beer can pop-top by some dude hawking his stuff outside a Stuckey's truck stop. But, of course, that's not quite right. Fixing up a house is not like proposing marriage or getting married, both of which are ceremonies, not actual relationships. If it didn't work out, shitty ring/countertop or not, we'd still be married. We were just running the risk of letting everybody know that the most conspicuous and arguably the most important ornament of our devotion to each other and our mutual institution — literally, figuratively, a rock — was a piece of shit. It'd take a lot of *Power of Positive Thinking* tapes to get us through that kind of fuckup. It wasn't exactly a foregone conclusion. You try explaining to your grandfather/benefactor why he should front a bunch of cash to an otherwise unemployed "artisan concrete worker."

"Concrete?" my grandfather said. "In your what? I hope you know what the hell you're talking about because I, for one, do not."

Predictably, I was of little help. I thought I might have been, because I had once spent a summer month working with my biological father in Alaska when he invited me up to get to know me. We laid concrete foundations for Coast Guard housing, and I thought that might translate into an impressive skill set as far as Steve was concerned, but that concrete and this concrete were two altogether different critters. In Alaska we were mostly gatekeepers, building plywood forms for somebody else to put the concrete in. And then, after it dried, we'd strip the plywood, set it up again fifty feet away, and repeat, ad nauseam.

What Steve did, however, was a minor work of art, albeit of the domestic cement variety. The second he showed up I knew I would be of little help. I knew it from the way he looked me square in the forehead like a boxer or a serial killer. I knew it from the fact that his tools were inherited, all older than both of us combined. I knew it too when he walked into my house for the first time and ten minutes later walked out with my big old L-shaped countertop all by himself.

My help consisted of making coffee (for myself — he was from Utah, after all) and keeping the radio tuned to the appropriate public radio station.

As a culture, we don't usually associate cement work with art, but maybe we should reconsider. Once our old countertop was removed, we were left with cabinets without lids. About twenty square feet of topless boxes. A kitchen without a countertop is like a garage without a driveway or a chair without legs. The space is essentially the same, but it's rendered useless. Without the countertop, the place looked plain wrong. Some things are better left unexperienced. To see a job in the middle of completion is like channel surfing and getting accidentally stuck on the Surgery Channel.

Steve saw not simply what was, but rather what could be. He imagined the final product and constructed the form that would render it possible. In effect, through three-quarter-inch plywood, angle iron, and custom-cut steel, Steve created a negative from which he could pour a positive. He took the negative space around what his imagination drew and used it to make the concrete manifest. It was a revelation.

The end result was glorious, concrete-y perfection. It was solid, smooth, and cool, and depending on the light, looked either like a rich, rare brown granite or like highly burnished English leather.

Also like firmly set chocolate pudding, as feared, but not in ways Jenae and I regretted. Nobody had seen anything like it. It was the best thing we did for the house. It was cheap, beautiful, and unique, and neither my bride nor I had to lift a finger.

In a couple of months, Steve and his wife and their newborn were going to move down to central Utah, where his father-in-law had some fifty acres of land, to see if they could live off the grid and raise produce and chickens and such all by themselves. Like Thoreau, apparently, Steve didn't want to make countertop art for the sake of turning it and thereby himself into an industry. He did it because it was something he wanted to do for himself and maybe for a few other people, so he would know what it takes to do it right.

The compulsion to repeat gratifying acts is so hard-wired in our brains that to find someone who is willing to give up something like this is truly befuddling. Then again, we're not talking about paper airplanes or peach cobbler. The fabrication of a concrete countertop is far from a Sunday-afternoon project, nor is it one a person undertakes so that he can kill a little time. It's as heavy duty as a project can get without involving front-end loaders or backhoes. If nothing else, a smart guy like Steve would have to know it's only a matter of time before one of those damned things would end up on his foot.

Behind the Confectionery

PREDICTABLY, A MONTH after Grandpa had moved in with my mom and Bob, I flew back to Wisconsin to help move him back out and into a new apartment. We decided to make it a "fun" trip for my mom and drive up together to Door County, Wisconsin's modest answer to Cape Cod. She hadn't had anything that resembled a break other than Grandpa's brief stay in the nursing home, and it had been a long and devastating year for all of us, but foremost for her. After we moved him into his place in downtown Waukesha — about two miles from my mom's condo — Mom and I couldn't wait to head up north, do a little golfing, and enjoy a few moments away from anyone named Bob.

We did not get our wish.

Despite the fact that Grandpa was as sick of Mom as he was of Bob, he felt left out and lonely as soon as he closed the door of his new apartment, and he said he was afraid he would go running to Tonya if left to his own devices for a whole weekend. So we were stuck. If we said no, we'd basically be begging him to get back with Tonya.

"I'll buy us all a nice dinner," he said.

Theoretically, change was possible.

We weren't ten miles north of Milwaukee when Grandpa's cell phone rang. No one has his number except my mom and Tonya. He's as good with his cell phone as a lobster with a hand grenade. It takes what seems like minutes for him to get it out of his coat pocket, and by then it stops ringing.

He catches me glaring at him in the mirror.

"I'd be happy to drive, Matt," he says, "if that's what's got you upset."

In the past year, he had torn his bumper off on a large rock in his condo subdivision, and then, shortly after he got new sunglasses and couldn't see, paradoxically, "because of the glare," he rear-ended a stopped car at forty miles per hour on Coffee Road. He'd had other accidents too, which he never told us about. All we know is that his car is as often as not in the body shop. Because of Grandpa's macular degeneration, cataracts, and glaucoma, we had hoped he would simply fail his license renewal test. But he passed. He doesn't have to get another vision test for seven years. Until he's nearly ninety.

"That's fine," I say. "I like to drive."

Crawling through traffic, up the coast of Wisconsin toward the Door County peninsula, feels like a long, elaborate walking of the plank. We're just north of Grafton now, the town where I spent my kindergarten and preschool years, about thirty miles north of Milwaukee. We still have a long drive ahead, and apparently nobody is going to reminisce with me.

Not too far from here, when I was a young boy, I fell out of my mom's VW van. Grandpa was driving. He was helping us move from an apartment on the north side of Milwaukee to a house in Grafton. We rolled up to a stop sign on a country road and the next thing I knew, I was on the pavement. The van had not quite stopped. My mom and grandma were driving behind us. Mom says it still wakes her up sometimes.

"I said I'd be happy to drive, Matt," Grandpa says.

"Thanks," I say, "Grandpa."

We all know, Grandpa included, that this is his fault. He and he alone is the occasion for our anger and unhappiness. Most semi-sentient creatures would understand when they are profoundly not wanted. Not my grandfather. He has never had a problem with enemies. It's friends and family he has never known what to do with.

"I am a licensed driver in the great state of Wisconsin," he says. "Maybe if you didn't make me move up here from Illinois you wouldn't have this problem. No way I would have passed their vision test."

"We didn't make you move to Wisconsin, Dad," my mom says. "And, Christ, that was two years ago. Mom was sick and you didn't want to pay for a full-time nurse and I couldn't quit my job and move down there and you didn't exactly have lots of friends to help out — "

"I know, I know." My grandfather laughs. "Jesus Christ."

He's jolly with meanness. It seems as though it's the last sure impact he can have on us. Tonya and her daughter can stroke his ego and God knows what else and let him pretend he's their sweet sugar daddy. My mom and I are bound to him in ways that remind me of Cronus, the Greek god who ate his children to prevent them from overthrowing him.

We're going about a hundred miles an hour before I realize it. I slow down to eighty. "How about some music?" I say, turning on the stereo.

"Good idea," my mom says. "I've got that new Alan Jackson album."

"One of Tonya's favorites," Grandpa says.

My mom turns off the stereo.

It's dark by the time we reach Door County. The drive takes about four hours, and most of it is on the freeway, but the last hour is on Highway 57 or 42, depending on whether you want to travel up the Green Bay or the Lake Michigan side. The peninsula itself is about eighty miles long. At its base, it's probably thirty miles wide, but it narrows as it moves north, so by the time you reach Valmy or Jacksonport, it's only about ten miles from shore to shore. We're not going that far, however. Cherry Hills is our destination. It's just a few miles outside Sturgeon Bay, right in the middle of Door County.

When we arrive, however, the resort looks deserted. There are no lights on in the dining room, and the main door to the reception area is locked.

My mom and I peer through the glass door, our hands cupped around our eyes. Grandpa teeters up and says, "What are you waiting for?"

"It's locked, Dad," my mom says.

"It's locked?" he says.

"Locked," I say. "As in not unlocked."

He's a little winded from the walk from the car. It's clear he has not fully recovered from his stroke — or, for that matter, his age. He just turned eighty-two. It is not nothing that he's outlived his wife by a year. No matter how complicated their life together must have been behind closed doors, she's still gone and he's still left, more or less alone, to deal with the fact that death came for the one we all thought should live forever.

"Well, did you make a reservation?" he says.

Try as I might to have pity for him, I don't. There's an after-hours phone number on the door, and I dial it on my cell phone and walk away. I realize simultaneously that this is what I do. To both of them, my mom and grandpa. They get worked up and I walk away. I am not proud, but neither am I turning around. Sometimes, I tell myself, I get to be the son and grandson before I have to be the man.

My mom and Bob used to own a condo in Sister Bay, right behind Al Johnson's restaurant — the one with the grass roof and the goats on it, across the street from the marina. When I was in college, I went up every chance I could. I liked going there alone, to read, write, and take pictures with my old manual Nikon FM2. After Christmas of my junior year, I went by myself for a day and a night. I read *A Portrait of the Artist as a Young Man* and was convinced I was reading my own autobiography. I didn't realize at the time that this made me a first-class wanker. I guess I still haven't. I'd rather read *Dubliners* than anything I've ever written or plan on writing. Even "Ivy Day in the Committee Room," whatever the hell that's about, but mostly "Araby," "The Sisters," and "The Dead." Oh, that perpetually soggy, dying Michael Fury and that never fully alive Gabriel. If only somebody could have gotten them together for Nora's sake. The day after I finished *Portrait,* I walked around in the clear bright cold air, taking pictures of coiled rope and a dead fish frozen on a pier that would be locked in ice for the next four months, hoping that if I put the image first, the meaning would follow. It was one of the coldest and best days of my life, not that I have the slightest clue what that fish meant.

At Cherry Hills, Grandpa and mom and I finally get our keys and go to our rooms to settle in, have a little nap and/or a cocktail before dinner. Mom and I are going to share a room and Grandpa

is going to stay in the adjoining room. Under different circumstances — such as "normal" circumstances — it would have been
more natural for me to stay with Grandpa. But it wasn't even a
question. In fact, he said so himself: "Can't hardly sleep through
the night. No sense in having us both be up all hours."

As soon as the door is shut between our rooms, I go to get ice,
come back, and mix a gimlet for my mom and a Scotch for myself — the last of Gram's once-formidable stash. We're just getting
ready to toast our "vacation" when Grandpa knocks. He decided
that he can't sleep at night because he takes too many naps during
the day, so maybe he had better stay up and have a cocktail with
us. Afterward, we can all go to dinner and then he'll turn in early. I
mix him a vodka on the rocks, and we sit on the beds facing different directions, not talking, not toasting to anything.

"Well, this is fun," he says.

"Yes, Dad, it sure was nice that you could come," my mom says.

He sighs, rattles the ice in his glass, and makes a big show of
slugging back the rest of his vodka.

"I'm on vacation," he says. "May as well have another."

This is never a good idea. But seeing as how his favorite target,
Bob, isn't here, maybe it'll help bring us all a little closer to wherever it is we need to be.

Grandpa's phone rings, and this time he manages to retrieve it
from his pocket while it's still ringing. "Excuse me," he says. He
goes into his room and announces officiously: "*Bob Tucker!*"

He doesn't manage to shut the door all the way behind him.
"Just fine, fine," he says. He's talking higher, wimpier. "And how are
you? I wish to Christ I could be there with you guys."

I get up and close the door, a little louder than I mean to.

"Makes me sick," my mom says.

I refill our drinks and we stare at the dark patio window as the sunset is replaced by our reflections.

"You know," she says, "fuck it." I'm shocked, but only as shocked as I can be given the circumstances. "If he wants to make her a part of this trip by being a sullen sonofabitch and always screwing around with his phone, fine."

Anything will be better than how things are going, I think. I wonder what she has in mind.

On the way to dinner, my mom says, "So, Dad, how's Tonya?"

I'm driving. We're headed north, practically to the tip of the thumb, as they call it, to a new restaurant in Ellison Bay.

"I didn't think you cared," he says.

"Well, I don't," my mom says, "but if you're going to be with us and always playing with your phone, pining away for her, you may as well talk about it."

This is as close as my mother has ever come to sarcasm.

"Well, fine," Grandpa says. "To tell you the truth, I miss the hell out of her and I wish I was with her."

The countryside we pass through is black. There is no traffic, no streetlights, no moon.

"Then why aren't you?" my mom says. "It's not like you're blessing us with your cheery mood and pleasant conversation."

I can feel my pulse behind my eyes. I know if I say anything we'll all blow up. I wring the steering wheel and try not to think about what would happen if I jerked it hard and took us into a steep ditch. I know just the place, a couple of miles south of Fish Creek. I can do something about all this, I realize. Dark, I admit. But some volition's better than nothing sometimes.

"I was supposed to be with her this weekend," my grandpa says.

"We were supposed to go to the Dells together with her kids. To that place we used to take you, Matt — the one with the water slides and the fake ark? — Noah's? — but something came up, and Tim, her ex-husband who's now her boyfriend again, insisted on being a part of it, and normally I wouldn't mind, but I just didn't feel like that would have been worth it. I mean, Tim and I get along fine, but, I don't know, I feel like he's trying to come between me and Tonya."

"Tim is — " I say. I can barely believe we're having this conversation. " — he's coming between you and Tonya?"

We pass through Egg Harbor and by the Alpine golf resort. I've been there a dozen times at least. I remember once we had Fairway with us and the German innkeeper sized him up like a schnitzel. "Hello, little doggie. Vhat is your name? Fairvay? Vhat a pretty name. Vhat a pretty little plump doggie you are."

"They have a very casual relationship," my grandfather continues. "An 'open relationship.' It's very European. I don't expect you to understand."

Never in my life have I needed a drink and a cigarette more than right now. I haven't had a smoke all day, and despite the fact that I've already had more Scotch than I should have, I feel altogether too sober to be hearing what I'm hearing. I force myself to stay between the ditches.

"Doesn't that give you a hint that maybe you shouldn't be a part of her life?" my mom says. She's staring straight ahead, as though if she turns around and looks at Grandpa in the back seat, she might find that he's totally naked.

"Oh, Jesus Christ," he says. He is beginning to cry. "I just love her too damned much." He slumps forward and his sobs rock my seat.

We pass by the Beowulf lodge, between Fish Creek and Sister

Bay. One summer, I remember, I practically lived there when my mom opened a business called Inkadinkadoo, which sold personalized stationery and rubber stamps. We would go up for long weekends so she could work, and I would spend half the day in the shop, playing with the rubber sheets of names with which she made the stamps, and try to come up with unique ways to blend inks into dark and strange rainbows. There were never any customers — her shop was across the street from the beach and behind the Confectionery, a great candy shop with wood casks overflowing with taffy and hard candy — and I would play with every stamp and come up with ways of telling stories, taking the pointer-finger stamp and making him go to the beach with the parasol stamp and the smiley-face sun stamp.

I wish the Confectionery were open tonight. We could use some hard candy. Gram always had some in her purse, and now I'm beginning to understand why. If you have to bite down hard on some kind of bit, might as well be a flavor of your choosing.

We pull up to the restaurant in silence.

"Dad," my mom says, helping him out of the car. It is neither a question nor a comment. It's something she can't do anything about.

Inside, we order a round of drinks as though our cocktails are our names and we're introducing ourselves to the waitress.

The restaurant is dark and woodsy with heavy beamed ceilings, and it feels as if we are the only people in the place. The menu has lots of interesting local fare that I don't dare try, given the lack of business this early in the season. Rainbow trout, walleyed pike, wild pheasant. We all order the filet mignon instead.

"Don't you want the prime rib, Patti?" my grandfather asks. He always makes a big show of insisting that my mom get prime rib.

"I don't really feel like it tonight, Dad," she says.

"Don't feel like prime rib?" He's never heard anything so preposterous.

We're sitting at a square table, with my mom and grandfather facing each other, me facing the seat where Gram should be. The seat Grandpa wants Tonya to be in. That's the issue, I realize. I knew we'd been living in the Year of the Empty Seat, but it didn't occur to me until just now that the problem wasn't the vacancy but whom we each wanted to fill the void.

"Did you get those steaks I sent you, Matt?" he asks.

I tell him yes and that I thought I had thanked him.

"What about the Bubba Burgers?"

I swirl the ice around my glass. He's still there when I look up.

"Thanks for the Bubba Burgers too," I say.

"If you don't like them, just say so," he says. "They don't send themselves, you know. I sure as hell don't have to."

I tell him I am aware of that. As it happens, we gave them away to our friends Steve and Julie, who just had a baby. Jenae hated those damned burgers. Frozen hamburgers stamped out in the vague shape of Texas is not something I need to find in my mailbox.

He turns to my mom with a bit of a cocky head-shake.

"How could anybody not feel like prime rib?" he says, though he himself didn't order it.

My mom doesn't answer. I don't say anything.

He sighs.

"Tonya doesn't like prime rib either," he says. "I guess you and Tonya have a lot more in common than you might like, Patti."

I am not a fighting man. Like most scrawny teenagers who grew up in the eighties watching Bruce Lee, Jackie Chan, and Chuck

Norris movies, I had a fleeting love affair with karate. Despite the rhetoric of inner peace, balance, and discipline that they sell to parents, all I ever got out of it were savage ass-kickings by lonely adults with acne scars and too much time between their shifts at Domino's. That, and a few promising but impractical seven-second death holds. My karate experiences explain a lot about my martial style. I either go down like a little pansy or punch you in the larynx. Guys I knew in school and around the neighborhood were always getting into fights for fun. They would bloody each other up and then walk over to the Dairy Queen together for Peanut Buster Parfaits as though nothing had happened.

"Excuse me?" my mom says.

Here we are, my mom and I, on vacation ostensibly to get away from Grandpa and all his bullshit, and he foists himself on us because his fair beloved decides she'd rather spend her weekend with someone she's already divorced from. And now, because Grandpa's all messed up with whatever it is he's going through, he decides to take it out on us, as though we're the ones being unreasonable.

"What the hell kind of a thing is that to say?" I ask. My speech is measured and precise. I have rarely blown up in real anger, never mind actually punched somebody in the throat, and I don't know that I'm looking forward to it.

"Well, I just think that your mom and Tonya have more in common than you realize."

"For Pete's sake, Dad," my mom says. The waitress drops off some bread and a bowl with butter that has been balled with an ice cream scoop. I throw back the rest of my Scotch and motion for another.

"You both like that new Alan Jackson album," he says, smiling.

"And then you both like cheap vodka. And Vegas — you both like Las Vegas. And me, right?" He's smirking, but he chokes back a sob. "You both love me, right?"

"Oh, for the love of God, Dad," my mom says. She digs into her purse, pulls out a Kleenex, and tucks in it Grandpa's hand. "What is the *matter* with you?"

"I'm leaving," he says. He gets up unsteadily from the table and fishes around in his pocket for his keys, thinking, apparently, that he drove. "Where the hell are they?" he says. "Did you take my keys?"

"What are you talking about?" I say. "We didn't take your car. You didn't drive. And you can't drive. You're in no condition to drive."

"What the hell do you know?" he says. "I'll do whatever I damned well please." He staggers backward, braces himself against his chair, turns around, and heads for the bar.

Just to make sure, I check my pocket. I have the keys. For a second I wonder what would happen if I let him have them. Would he solve the problem that he has become?

"In a million years," Mom says, "I never would have thought it would come to this."

She stands up, tosses her napkin aloft, and goes to fetch her father. The napkin catches the air momentarily, like a little parachute. Or a flag of surrender.

The waitress returns with my Scotch. "Everything all right?" she says.

"Dandy," I say. "Just keep 'em coming."

After a few minutes, Mom returns with Grandpa. She has her arm around his hunched shoulders, looking like a Red Cross volunteer delivering aid to the victim of a natural disaster, not a daughter returning her father to a table at a nice restaurant in a popular vacation destination. All they're missing is the scratchy gray wool blanket and a little white nurse's cap for mom.

I am grateful we didn't bother ordering appetizers. Our waitress brings our steaks out on a tray. She sets it down next to our table and stands back, trying to determine if she can safely negotiate our theatrics, but we're drained for the time being, so she tucks our plates in front of us and scoots away.

"I just love her too damned much," he says and has been saying. He's trying to cut his steak, but with his poor eyesight and the low light he can't tell he's using the wrong side of his knife. "Too goddamned much," he says.

My mom takes his plate from him, cuts up his steak in little cubes, and puts it back in front of him.

"I am so thankful that Gram is not around to see this," she says to no one in particular.

No one can find any of our three room keys. After all we've had to drink, we're lucky we got back to the hotel at all, but getting there and not being able to get in is no relief whatsoever.

"You don't have the key, Patti?"

My grandpa is thoroughly confused, lost.

"*No,* Dad," my mom says. "*Nobody* has the *key.*"

Everything we say tonight is addled with italics.

"I thought you had the key," he says. "I had mine a minute ago. Didn't we just do this? Weren't we just here?"

We're standing outside the hotel, it's about eleven o'clock at night, and it's dark and colder than you might expect in May. There are a couple more cars in the parking lot, but it still looks as if we're more or less alone in this place.

I walk to the main door, but it's locked again and my cell phone is in the room.

Surprisingly, I am not nearly as drunk as I want to be. I need a cigarette and some time to myself, at, say, a Franciscan monastery, but instead I am trapped outside our hotel room with my mom and grandfather, facing the prospect of sleeping in the Hyundai with them.

Then I remember the patio. Before we went out to dinner, we left the sliding door open to air the place out.

"I'll be right back," I say.

I jog around the dark end of the hotel, toward the eighteenth green. Cherry Hills is built into the hillside, making the parking lot and the entrance on the second floor, so out back I'm a story below our rooms. The only light in all of Door County is coming from our windows.

I jump up on the railing of the first-floor room and find that I am a couple of inches too short to reach the bottom of our porch. I prop myself against the beam and figure it's either jump and hold on like hell or sleep in the car and bicker all night long.

I jump.

Fortunately, I've been rock climbing enough in Utah (much as everyone in Utah is a Mormon by osmosis, so too are we all climbers and backcountry skiers). I'm not much of a lead climber, but I really hate falling, so I'm pretty good at hanging on. The metal of the rail is cold, and I can feel it flex a little too much under the strain of my weight. I realize only as I bounce with the inertia from my jump that this is not what these decorative metal railings are made for. After having done all the work on the house, I also realize — a bit too late — that these rails are probably installed with inch-and-a-half screws into wood that has been exposed to the elements for years. In other words, there's a good chance that I'll rip the whole railing off the porch and end up wearing it on my face, like a grotesquely oversize set of braces.

But I don't. I commit to my little operation and swing my feet up, get them under me, and stand up on our porch. I turn around before I go inside and watch the late-spring clouds sliding darkly across the sky like a network of scenery screens changing between the acts of a play. They move steadily and quickly, one in front of the other, and the dim new moon appears to be amid them and not where it really is — far, far away.

I go inside, grab the key, and retrieve what's left of our family.

We sit watching Letterman at a volume that makes my teeth ache. We want to talk. We want to say things. We want to have things to say, but we don't.

"I hope they're having more fun than I am," Grandpa says during a commercial for a new antacid.

I do not ask what he means. I know. He has only one subject left. It's Tonya. Tonya and Tim. Tonya and Daphne. Tonya and her children. Tonya and her grandchildren. Tonya and her Mitsubishi. Tonya and her Harley-Davidson dreams. Tonya and her Jägermeister shooters. Tonya and her Alan Jackson. Tonya and her morals.

He starts crying again. His sobs shake his body, and only the ice jingles sympathetically in his glass. He gets up and leaves the room. He does not use the adjoining door.

I know for a fact that he doesn't have a key. I let him leave.

My mom has fallen asleep and doesn't stir even when the door slams behind Grandpa. She's slumped in a side chair with a low back, and her head is tilted at such an unnatural angle that she appears to have fractured her spine.

Finally. I can go out to smoke. I pick up my phone, grab the almost empty bottle of Scotch and my rolling tobacco, and slide out the same way my grandfather left. He's nowhere in sight and I really don't care. I feel toxic and evil and over it all.

"Wish you were here," I say on the phone to Jenae. "The weather's beautiful."

She knows it's not funny. She knows it has to be *bad*.

"Get good mileage?" she says.

For the first time since I arrived, I laugh.

I roll a cigarette, an affectation for which I have little use tonight. My hands are shaking, I'm so tense and agitated. The tobacco keeps spilling off the paper, disappearing into the gravel of the parking lot.

I imagine her, back in Salt Lake, curled up on our overstuffed red couch — the one we got from Grandpa when he moved out of his condo. We don't particularly care for it; Tonya and Grandpa picked it out together because Gram was too sick to shop for a couch to make her more comfortable.

I light the cigarette, inhale, and almost fall over from the rush. Every cell in my body at once deflates and then puffs back up in a wave of chemical adjustment. It is not, nor does it feel, healthy.

Jenae asks me where I am. She sounds concerned. I imagine she should be.

"I'm sitting in the parking lot with my cigarettes and not nearly enough booze to get me through this night."

I know it sounds ugly. It was. If only there were spent shell casings, dirty needles, and ransom notes to tell about too.

"Oh, honey," Jenae says. She means it. This is what she is best at. The kind of comfort that keeps me alive.

But she's too far away to do anything about where I am for more than the time being, and I want to cry, to scream, to get ripping drunk. I want to fight. I want to kick and punch and bite and claw my way through to something that will pass for the truth. I want to find the truth and head-butt it in the nose, sending bits of its broken nasal bone back into its brain like bright streaking meteors irreparably penetrating all that mushy gray matter once and for all. I want to hit my grandfather between the eyes and tell him he is a fucking moron and he's destroying what little remains of our family. I want *damage*.

"Please don't go anywhere tonight," Jenae says. "You don't sound well."

I finish off the rest of the Dewar's in a swallow, take the bottle by the neck, and rear back to chuck it over the hotel.

But I don't throw it. Despite my rage, I'm too worried about the prospect of somebody being there — somebody who happens to be practicing his putting at midnight or walking his little Jack Russell on the golf course, looking for lost balls. And then there's the whole prospect of the bottle breaking and then there would be this broken glass all over the eighteenth green and somebody would have to pick it up and it would be a pain in the ass and they would hate themselves and their boss and their job and their lives because that is what it all comes down to: some sorry kid from Waukesha can't get his shit together and so he's got to make life onerous for everybody else.

I set the empty bottle down on the pavement and start crying. It does not feel like relief.

"Oh, baby," Jenae says. "Baby."

After a few more cigarettes I go back inside. Grandpa is moving away from his door, back toward the deserted reception area. He's shuffling his feet, barely picking them up, and it makes me feel violent all over again.

"What are you doing?" I say. It's not as mean as I want it to be.

He looks up, sees nothing but darkness ahead of him, then realizes that it's me and that I am behind him. He turns around. It's very metaphoric.

"My key," he says.

"I know," I say. "You don't have one. Where the hell have you been this whole time?"

His shirt is untucked and there is either water or spit dribbled down the front.

"I," he says. "I . . ."

"Hush," I say and take him to his room.

Everyone is in bed, but I cannot bear to close my eyes or otherwise finesse my way to sleep. It is 1:47 A.M. and then it is 1:53 A.M. and all I can do is count my blinks. I do not want to watch TV. I do not want to read. I am not drunk, but neither am I sober. I want nothing. I want a void. I contemplate giving myself what I would hope to be a partial lobotomy with a Ticonderoga number 2 pencil. It is 2:28. It is 2:36. I want safe passage to morning, but it is apparently too late to buy a ticket. It is 2:48. It is 2:48. It is 2:48.

I manage to stay in bed until just before five. I cannot think of the last time I woke up this early. Not by *hours*. But nothing could lull me into sleep this night. There is stillness in Grandpa's room. My mom is silent in her chair. She has not moved all night. I forget: this is different only in venue from her usual tedium with Grandpa. This is her life.

I am such a dick.

I put on shorts and a T-shirt, grab a key, and leave. The sound of the door closing behind me is sweet as a first kiss.

Beyond the sulfur lights of the maintenance shack, the night is the color and consistency of ink. I do not know where I am going. I know only that I have got to get away, for at least a while, lest I do someone or something grievous harm. I run.

I turn left out of the parking lot and am immediately blinded as my eyes try to make the harsh adjustment from the bright lot to the unlit, now moonless predawn. It feels as though I have been cast from a ship, jettisoned into space or sea — I don't have sufficient sensory evidence yet to tell which. To my right a horse whinnies, then another, a smaller snuffle. A colt, I think, I hope. I run, trusting the gravel shoulder to tell me when I've strayed from the road. The air smells green and fecund, like wet grass, sweet manure, and freshwater fish.

I run uphill in the dark, and as the light begins to change, I can tell that there are woods on either side of me, open water ahead. My lungs hurt from smoking, and my kidneys throb with pain from a lack of water and an excess of Scotch, but I have no time for apologies. If I can't find somebody to hit me in the face so my body and mind are at least feeling the same thing, then I have got to do it myself.

I reach a crest and am going downhill fast and it's hard on my knees and I'm trying to let the hill ease me down but there's something brutal and honest about running fast downhill. And then I'm at the water — the bay — and I head north and run as fast as I can. I try to condense everything into a singular seed of pain and then try to run harder to blow off the husk so there is nothing left but the raw, red, meaty hurt. The light comes from my right, over the trees, and the water stays dark and tempting for a long time, almost an hour, I figure, until I have gone as far as I can and reasonably expect to return. Even I know: I have to return. There is a continental breakfast to be had, danishes and little globes of cantaloupe and cream-cheese-filled kringles and sausage and bacon. Bacon, the only true consolation the day has for the night.

I stop. In the middle of the road. Somewhere a few miles north of Sturgeon Bay. Where woods and water meet. I stagger down through the grass, across the narrow beach, and into the still water, where I stare at my reflection like a dead flower. I splash my face and shatter my image. I know if I wait, it will come together again. It might even be a face I recognize.

I don't. I run, a little less hard, but it's just as punishing. The day warms and the sun comes up over the trees, but I know it is still remarkably early.

And then, at the base of the hill I almost hit something in the road. A snake, and it's bigger than I ever imagined a Wisconsin reptile could be, but there it is. Dead. I grab a stick and poke it, just to make sure.

I will it to mean something — to stand for something — but there are no more metaphors for anything, not in Wisconsin, not this early in the morning.

Finish, Carpenter!

JUST WHEN THE HOUSE begins to feel like a real place of our own, the washing machine learns to walk. We would start an ordinary load of clothes, and by the time it gets to the first spin cycle, the machine would be halfway across the room before I can catch up with it, its hot and cold water hoses straining to keep it from jumping down the stairs. As badly as I wish for the machine to be the problem, we know it's bigger and badder than that. It's the foundation.

The original structure was built in 1911, and while it was obviously solid enough to last nearly a hundred years, it's beginning to show its age in ways that keep me up at night more than any worries did about my grandfather's lower GI or romantic depravity. There is a crack in the foyer wall that I can fit a pencil in, and another gap between the dining room floor and wall big enough to fit a dictionary. Outside, there are growing fissures between some of the bricks, evidence of a tectonic-scale struggle on the part of the house to stay on the lot. Downstairs, however, is where things get scary.

The laundry room comes off the kitchen in what had once been an unfinished porch. We want to extend the slate floor through there, but something is obviously wrong with the room. A closer inspection below reveals a disaster on par with the rest of Stanley's construction finery: he has used lumber apparently salvaged from a chemical fire to build the foundation for the laundry room. Two-by-four wall studs, I find out, are supposed to be spaced sixteen inches apart, with the skinny, two-inch part facing you and the wide, four-inch parts facing each other. They studs are supposed to be in a line front to back, as though they were soldiers marching forward. Stanley's soldiers are facing the other direction — shoulder to shoulder, as it were — a bunch of seditious traitors standing before a firing squad. The problem with aligning them that way is that you can only rest a two-inch board on top to frame the wall and not the four-inch header it needs. In short, it's bad. We have a fifty-square-foot floor, a staircase, a washer and a dryer, and two bookcases with about ten years and a thousand pounds of Martha Stewart magazines and cookbooks — all of it propped up on some charred and rotten sticks topped with quarter-inch plywood through which the dappled daylight shines.

Adding another seven or eight hundred pounds of rock on that floor isn't something I felt super-cozy about. I call our friend Erik and bribe him with his favorite Jamaican beer to come over to take a look under the hood.

"Jesus, dude," he says, "this is messed up." Instinctively he covers his head. "This whole floor is being held up by what are basically furring strips. House of cards, man. How the hell did this pass inspection?"

I point to a large, three-quarter-inch piece of plywood that has been shimmed in place beside the stairs. The rise and run of the stairs are far from regulation, and as you get to the bottom, if you are not chronically stooped, you had damned well better pay attention to the header on which you are about to smack your noggin. The inspector probably never knew what he was missing.

"Weak," Erik says.

He goes to the east wall and says it looks all right. The same with the north wall. But when he gets to the staircase, he freezes.

Erik looks at me, then back to the square post upon which the staircase sits.

"Are you messing with me?" he says. "Did you do this?"

"Do what?" I don't even know what I am looking at. It just looks like the shabby underside of a staircase.

Erik points to the post. It is not a post. It's three different pieces of wood. The base of it is a four-by-four, as it should be, but on top of it are two two-by-fours, sistered together and wedged between the top of the post and the bottom of the stairs.

Essentially, what you want in a beam like this is a stout, solid leg. Instead of the fully muscled leg of a power lifter, we have a horror show from the chop shop of Victor Frankenstein. The prosthetic equivalent supporting our entire laundry room floor would have looked like an intact though severely atrophied foot and calf, but then, above the knee, the thigh of two other bodies. Sutured and stapled together with the artistry of a maniacal but massively thrifty necromancer is the hamstring from one badly decayed corpse and the quadriceps from what might have been a healthy child had polio not set her musculature to waste.

"Dude," Erik says. He is serious.

With one hand, Erik pushes up on the stairs and, with the other, wiggles the post clear out from under the tread. "Nice," he says. "Super."

It is going to take a lot of Red Stripe to fix this.

* * *

Erik and I walk to the lumber section of Home Depot, back by the uncouth area reserved for professionals. The rest of the place bristles with catchy signs and flashy brochures soliciting the weekender warriors' attention. *Make over your breakfast nook into a neat nest fast! Turn that seventies shag into contemporary chic!* Their Sirens sing of speed, ease, and savings. They sell projects to the unwary with promises of simplicity and increased self-esteem. *You CAN do it!* they swear. *WE can help!* Never mind that the average shopper in a place like this is simply looking for a three-prong adapter, a squeegee, and sundry other things to cover up why he really came, which is for yet another toilet seat after that debacle last week at your Super Bowl party.

Back in the lumber section, however, things are different. The aisles are wide and completely unadorned, with no signs, promises, directions, or piped-in music. just stacks upon stacks of raw lumber. Sawdust sweeps around the floor, and lone contractors mosey along the aisles with squeaky-wheeled carts laden with wood and fasteners. The men in this section of the store wear silver tape measures on their belts, utility knives and pliers tucked in leather holsters. They swagger down the rows seeming to know precisely what they're looking for, but they aren't in a hurry because they're on a dedicated run to get the stuff to finish whatever job they had just escaped, invariably a time-and-materials deal where one of the only benefits is milking the clock while shopping around for the right piece of wood, eating a Polish sausage bought from the halter-topped gal at the lunch cart by the entrance.

Erik and I are wearing shorts and flip-flops. We look as if we have just finished cutting a surf-rock album and are lost looking for some charcoal for our hibachi. Erik is professionally casual, however, whereas I am ignorantly harried. I feel that we need a license or a special dispensation from Glendon or another higher authority to be allowed in this part of the store. Erik, of course, knows better and has the walk down, regardless of his lack of a tool belt. He grabs a tape measure from a display and walks right up to a bin of a hundred twelve-foot two-by-fours.

"I thought we needed six-footers?" I say. I feel a little giddy being able to say something like that and not be talking about reasonably hard putts or semi-crippled spiders.

Erik doesn't look at me. He takes a board from the stack, swings it out, drops one end on the ground, and holds the other close to his eye as if he is sighting a rifle or preparing to play one of those Swiss alpine horns.

"We'll cut them in half," he says, tossing the board on a flat metal cart. "More money for beer."

Erik is my kind of genius. He takes another board, turns that one over. Instead of putting it in the cart, he throws it back into the bin. I am mystified.

A big dude with American flag suspenders walks by, checking us out as though wondering how gratifying it would be to chain us to a fence. Erik picks up another two-by-four, spins it in his hand while again sighting down the board, and tosses it nonchalantly on the cart. The suspendered dude walks on back toward the manufactured lattice.

"The way they store and ship lumber is more often than not on uncovered railroad cars and open-air semis," Erik says. "All the wood on the outside is exposed for weeks or months to rain and snow and sun and so forth. It's all been kiln-dried, but it's still wood. The shit warps."

He takes another piece and hands it to me. No way I'd have an eye for this, I think, imagining it to be as difficult as worrying about such nonsense as windage and elevation when aiming a rifle, but instead I hold it up and it's clear: there is a pretty ugly bend toward the end of the board.

What was mysterious and ineffable a moment ago is suddenly obvious and all but self-explanatory. The real mystery is why this happens so often to me.

Once we're in my basement again, I ask Erik if we hadn't best be wearing helmets. He is poised to prop up the laundry room floor with a couple of two-by-fours so we can tear out the old beam and insert a good new one. If we are going to be buried beneath a house, I want to give my head a fighting chance at survival. I put on my climbing helmet and give Erik my beat-up bike helmet. He puts it on backward and the chin straps hang down like pigtails.

Before becoming immersed in the renovation, I thought a house was a complete structural whole — an *entity* — none of which could be compromised or altered without risking the integrity of the whole shebang. As we tear away layer after layer of what are essentially cosmetics, I find my life is working in much the same way. Jenae and I aren't merely coexisting in the same crappy apartment anymore, we are *living* together. We're hanging out more, talking to each other, going on hikes — even a climb or two — really *being* a couple. Now that we have something to invest in, we are constantly reinventing ourselves, our surroundings, our lives together. We aren't sloughing off responsibility or blaming our inadequacies on our surroundings or our station in life; we are taking inventory, making plans, stripping paint, and swinging hammers. If we don't like something, we immediately set about finding ways to revise it. One morning we think it'd be nifty to put a path from the back door to the garage, and by noon we are off in the desert mountains west of the Great Salt Lake harvesting unsuspecting rocks and piling them in the old Land Cruiser until the leaf springs about pop. It isn't easy — none of it is — but it is good work. We have made an investment and we are going to see it through.

Still, we know we have only begun to round the learning curve. My great fear is that the real lessons will come in the shape of a catastrophe. Salt Lake City, after all, is situated on top of a fault. As a rule of thumb, you don't get mountains without some serious seismic activity. Just the thought of a small earthquake and those palsied, weak wood beams in our basement make me, well, tremble.

"All right," Erik says, "hello? Where'd you wander off to? Do I have to keep you on one of those toddler leashes? Christ, dude. You gotta keep your head in this." He has finished fitting the temporary braces into place and is ready for Lord knows what kind of collaboration. "So, I think these'll do the trick. Push."

I stand below the staircase and push up on the ceiling as hard as I can. I am both emboldened and disturbed that I am actually able to lift the ceiling off its foundation. Erik slips a two-by-four underneath and hammers the base home. I let my arms go slack and the board he just put in place bows out dramatically. I straighten back up and realize I won't be pinch-hitting for Atlas anytime soon.

"Don't worry," Erik says. "Need another one just a bit longer. Sit tight."

With a little too much aplomb, he hops on the stairs and climbs up and over my head and the stairs I am supporting.

"Dude," I say. "Dude?"

"Relax," he yells from outside. "I mean, you know, don't *relax* relax, but relax."

I hear the saw spark to life and then the wail of the blade on wood. I know he is working fast and I know he is doing it right, but it takes a lot more than that to make somebody feel at peace while he's holding up the better part of his house.

Erik walks back over my hands and drops down into the basement. "You're not getting tired, are you?"

"Seriously," I say.

With a few swift strokes Erik fits the other support in and I feel a little less stress on my hands.

He smiles and looks at me. "How long are you going to stay like that?"

"I mean," I say, "I can still feel a little pressure."

"Baby," Erik says, "that's homeownership."

He shrugs and starts measuring the remaining two-by-fours to frame in the rest of the job. We have the other three walls to reinforce, and perhaps a central beam to add, but we (Erik) have strengthened the weakest part of the structure.

"I feel pretty good about it," Erik says.

"Pretty good?" I say. Travis, a climbing buddy of mine, had once called a piton he found "marginal"; nevertheless, we clipped into it and descended a few stories back to earth. About a month later, the piton blew and I heard a couple of good climbers ended up dead. Coming out of Erik's mouth, "pretty good" inspired even less confidence than "marginal."

"Check it," he says. Out of habit, I am still sort of holding up the ceiling. Erik drops his hammer and jumps back up above my head. "Ready?"

Before I can say "For what?" Erik hops up and down on the landing above me. The floor flexes and shakes as dirt and rotten wood rain from the beam in my hands, but miraculously it doesn't give.

"Yeah, not bad," Erik says. "I gotta get to work, so, you know, you might check out a laundromat until we finish this thing off proper."

No argument ensues.

Erik has his own work over the next few days, but he assures me that I can do the rest myself. All I have to do is get a couple of "hanger brackets" to nail into the existing "support beams," "pressure fit" new "treated two-by-fours" into them, set up a couple of "headers," "frame in" the rest of the walls, and then I'd be set. Of course, first I have to figure out how to take the quotation marks off all the directions I wrote down from Erik.

Bolstered by our initial success, I go back to the store by myself. I march in, with what might as well be a Hello Kitty tape measure on my belt, and go straight to the stacks of two-by-fours. I imitate Erik's process of selection as best I can, sighting down the lengths of boards as though I am blowing glass. I am just glad nobody in double-wide suspenders is lurking about that day to test my resolve.

I get back home and begin the measuring and cutting without any trouble. Then again, you can measure and cut wood all day long and unless you sever a digit you'll never know you fucked up until it comes time to fit the pieces into place. Erik had cut everything so quickly and then poetically toenailed the boards together — getting nails to bend as if by volition alone. When I get downstairs, however, and begin to see how ragged and inaccurate some of my cuts are, I feel it's too late to do anything about it. I am mad and want to be finished with this damned project, so I pick up a heavy, waffle-faced framing hammer, thinking that with its additional heft I should be able to drive nails as easily into lumber as into sponge cake. But this hammer is a professional's tool, and I am as prepared to use it as a Red Rider–wielding seven-year-old is a twelve-gauge shotgun. I brutalize the wood and the nails alike. One particular nail takes me ten minutes to drive because I can only reach it upside down with my left hand — I may as well have tried to push it in with my tongue.

Despite that, I love this work because I love the tools. And no tool enjoys a greater marriage of form and purpose than a hammer. It looks precisely like what it is. You pick it up and your hand knows just what it's for. The smooth, shiny, slightly aerodynamic face and the claw on the back resembling an arrow's fletching — it's so beautiful you want to swing it hard and hit something again and again and again, *pock pock pock,* until the nail is driven home and the timber tight and your point well made. It's brutality at its most elegant. In my hands, sadly, it is as useful as flaccid asparagus for driving long, sixteenpenny nails into fresh wood.

Still, *still,* I am doing it. I am framing walls, studs sixteen inches center-to-center. I am sistering weak, compromised beams with fresh, good wood. I hang brackets and pressure-fit everything the way Erik said, so that when weighted with a new slate floor and a full forty-gallon-capacity washing machine sloshing around with jeans and corduroys in it, the floor will hold steady. I go the extra distance and drill four holes through stone and bolt a bracket to the cement floor for a four-by-four-inch beam to take the majority of the weight off the weaker perimeter and distribute the load more evenly.

It is tedious work that, if I do it right, no one will ever even think of. If I do it poorly or if it fails in some catastrophic way, all the blame will be mine. I understand now why Stanley had cut so many corners, but I can't permit myself to do the same. I want to do the right thing for us and the house.

It just deserves to be done right.

* * *

I move the washer and dryer into the kitchen and hunker down to tear up the old linoleum and subfloor in the laundry room. I dread the prospect of another tedious, all-day job, the way the kitchen floor had been, but instead I find that the linoleum in the laundry room wasn't even fixed to the floor. I simply pull up at a corner, peel it back, roll it up as if it's some foul yoga mat, and chuck the thing out the door.

I am not disappointed in Stanley anymore, nor am I surprised. I am just relieved that the bad job he did this time didn't manifest itself in that sorry mix of haste, thrift, and the wanton use of industrial adhesives he'd employed before.

I am so smug. I'm sure the neighbors are talking. The home-and-garden folks will be by any minute. After that, maybe a quick interview with Tommy Silva on *This Old House* and a cameo with Norm Abram on *The New Yankee Workshop*. Even though I am not much of a finish carpenter, when it comes to renovation per pound, I think I can weigh in with the best of them. At the very least, I can joke about that double-entendre "finish carpenter." Maybe even triple-entendre, if you mess with the spelling and capitalization.

I get a couple of pieces of plywood measured, cut, and screwed down. Before the drill is even cool, I have laid out the backerboard and fasten it into place. I butter up and seal the joints and am ready to lay some slate. I spin out the tiles like a blackjack dealer, figuring out what I need to do for the cut tiles on the border and around the ductwork. Next I go to Home Depot, have a little chitchat with my boy Glendon, rent the saw, make the cuts, return the saw ("Whoa, buddy," Glendon says, "already? Did you even leave the parking lot?"), go back home, whip up a bunch of thinset, slather it on, and lay out the tiles. I am ready for my Blue Ribbon of the Pabst variety by nightfall.

I crack open a beer and go around back to admire my work from outside, only to find a little problem.

I didn't do a thing with the stairs.

The critters in question are a set of L-shaped stairs with only ten treads, total, but they have a landing interrupting them where they meet the back door. So if you come into the house from outside, you'd turn immediately left and hike up three steps to the laundry room. Or, back at the door, you could go straight down seven treads and you'd be in the basement. The landing between them is about three square feet, just big enough for your boots and the decision you have to make, whether it's straight down or left and up.

They are stable now, to be sure, but they're as ugly as hell. Especially since they are the first thing you see when you come in from the backyard. I didn't notice them before because the floor was so bouncy it kept your vision dodgy. But now that we have the slate down, it runs right up to the edge of the back stairs and it is impossible not to see the paint and grease all over them, not to mention the errant hammer blows and pulverized nail heads and exposed joints.

Ideally, I could dismantle the stairway and build a new one — make the treads, say, and calculate the right rise and run so that people wouldn't concuss themselves on their way to the basement. Bang that sucker out in an afternoon and have it all tiled up by the time it was beer o'clock.

The problem with stairs, however, is that there is no room for guesswork, particularly where I am working. And, of course, this is the kind of structural carpentry you need a license and a permit for, neither of which I am likely to get in this lifetime.

I decide then and there, sitting on my crappy back staircase drinking cheap domestic mule piss only someone from Milwaukee can pretend to enjoy, I am going to pull a Stanley.

I try to forgive myself before I commit the sin upon which I am intent, but I know full well that trying to preempt absolution implies premeditation, and thereby secures the cardinal nature of the sin.

Because I have already dumped out the last of the thinset, I take the remaining slate tiles and slather them with the only adhesive I have left: caulk. I don't know why I don't wait until the next day and go to the store and get more thinset or Stanley-strength Liquid Nails and do it right, or at least right-er. In the big picture, I have already spent hundreds of hours on the renovations; what will another hour or two matter? As reasonable as that argument goes, nothing can persuade me to do it right and not be finished with it tonight. I want to be done with this job at any cost, even if it means never really being done, because I do it with the wrong materials at the wrong time of day on surfaces poorly prepped — and as a result I am left with a staircase that Stanley would have been proud of. It is done, but ugly, and whoever wants to do it right knows just where to start.

3

Rescue the drowning and tie your shoe-strings.

—THOREAU, 1854

Watershed

WE ARE DONE. Not finished, as my high school English teacher would remind us was correct, but done — as he would say, like chicken. We own a house we fixed up ourselves, and somehow we haven't fucked it up. It is miraculous.

Every morning, I get up and walk Maggie to the dog park down the street while Jenae gets ready for work. I let Skillet out back, and he will almost always climb too far up a tree and end up meowing pathetically to be rescued. Jenae works at the theater and I teach a few classes and wait tables, so our evenings and weekends usually involve sometimes fabulous and sometimes horrifying civic- and art-oriented duties. When nothing grand is going on, I cook our dinner of kabobs, a Mexican-ish thing, or any number of dishes with meatballs. Jenae walks Maggie and tries to teach Skillet how to use the toilet while I putter in the kitchen, and then we sit down in the family room to eat and watch a little TV — invariably, it seems, something involving impossibly witty cops, sanguine robbers, and hot, well-endowed scientists. Jenae reclines on the big red couch with Skillet, and Maggie corkscrews herself in the armchair, leaving me to sit cross-legged on the floor in front of her. It is perfect.

Above the TV we hang an old schoolhouse map of the United States, and in between bites of food or conversation, I stare at the faded primary-colored states, thinking about all the places we've been and where we still have friends, and I imagine where we might possibly end up and whether it will even be on that map. Utah is beautiful and austere, but like most other places, it's not for everybody. Moreover, in my line of work you don't get to stay where you go to school unless you don't mind using your degree to sling steaks. So, to give the thing a shot, on the job market I go. I know it will be years before anything like a real position comes our way anyway.

Or, as it turns out, not. We haven't been in the house three years when I get an offer from a bunch of midwestern expatriates teaching creative writing at a state school in Nacogdoches, Texas. I wouldn't have accepted so readily had not the town been mentioned in songs by both Steve Earle and Lucinda Williams, as well as in Cormac McCarthy's cheery gorefest, *Blood Meridian*. It's only a couple of hours away from Bruce in Houston, too. On top of it all is the fact that you never know whether you're ever going to get another job offer to do what you're trained to do — not even in the darkest depths of Texas.

What the hell. We're going to give it a shot.

Before we get ready to sell the house, we discover that Stacey, Jenae's roommate from Boston, is living in Sugarhouse, just three blocks away. (Sugarhouse really is one of only two possible neighborhoods for non-Mormons to live in the entire state, so it isn't really *that* unusual.) She actually just sold her house, in fact, and recommends a realtor whom she found easy to work with. He sold her place the day it went on the market. "It was too much money," Stacey says, still stunned. "Too much."

The realtor's name is Bob Plumb, and I ask Stacey if he is for real. "Bob Plumb, as in the reverse of a plumb bob, the thing you use to check if something is vertical?"

"With your name," Stacey says, "I wouldn't think you'd want to be casting any stones."

We've seen the Plumb For Sale signs around our neighborhood and up in The Avenues too, usually on homes we weren't qualified to clean, never mind own. We expect Bob to hand us off to some slobby, mouth-breathing underling, but he is the one who shows up in the requisite white luxury sedan (an unlikely Acura) to see the house.

"Hey guys! What's up, what's happening, what's going *on?*" he says, fast as a weed whacker. "You must be Jenae and you must be the guy and what a great location and man, that rose bush I remember this house when that was a tree — I grew up a few blocks from here and I've always liked this place. What did you say your name was?"

I say Matt Batt.

He pauses, making sure I am not fooling with him, perhaps affording me the space to explain that no, my parents weren't trying to set me up for a life of despair, it was just that my mom's second husband adopted me and so on and so forth. He thinks better of it, and we proceed.

He is a short man in his late forties or early fifties. He wears a lilac polo shirt, pressed khaki pants, and shoes with tassels. I don't need to see his credentials.

He holds out his hand. "Bob Plumb," he says. "And yeah, I've heard 'em all so give it a shot if you need to, but the bar has recently been set at 'Plumb Bob Scary Pants.' You either get it or you don't — I see you don't — anyway. Call me Bob."

I don't really need another Bob in my life, but what choice do I have? I shake his hand.

"I know, right," he says, "I get it. Slow down, Bob, right? It's okay, man. Matt, you said? Okay. Slowing down." It is like watching a hummingbird on amphetamines.

We go inside and Jenae gives Bob the tour as I trail behind. Since our last realtor experience, I didn't plan on trusting anybody farther than I could throw him, but I have to admit that Bob is kind of a little guy, and I might in fact be able to toss him farther than I expected.

"Hey, holy cow," he says, turning around to keep me in the fold, "you guys did this work? You're kidding, right? You must have had a lot of help, right? Holy cow, the colors! And good gravy, this hardwood floor, I mean, I know it's old and beat up, but they're paying fifty grand up in Park City for people to make new floors look like this one."

I notice, much to my chagrin, that the collar of his shirt is up. It could have been an accident — the wind, say — but still.

We sit down at the dining room table and talk about our plans and the market and what we are hoping to get out of the house. Bob laughs and rambles with Jenae as though they're old sorority sisters, but he keeps trying to draw me into the conversation too, not by being smarmy but by addressing as directly as he can my transparent mistrust of realtors.

"It's okay, Matt," he says, "I get it. You're nervous. You should be. Maybe not nervous — how about cautious? — because I know better than anybody lots of realtors are schnooks and shysters. But give me a chance, okay? Don't be a hater."

Jenae and I look at each other.

"My boy, the Lizard King — that's his skater name, not mine, but I kinda like it, nice throwback to the day, you know, the Doors? — anyway, my kid, LK, he came up with that one last night at the Spaghetti Factory — I take the whole family out, dad, grand-dad, all the kids — even the Lizard King's new girlfriend who was clearly a little freaked out by all us Plumb people and LK told her, 'Hey, baby, stop hatin' on us. Don't be a hater. Be a lover,' and so come on you two — I can see plain as the shine on my shoes you're lovers. Why you gotta be hatin' on Bob?"

He stops for just long enough to raise his eyebrows.

"Seriously," he says, "this is a great market and a great house and you guys are going to kill it. What do you guys want to get out of it?"

Jenae and I haven't really decided. I know she was hoping, in her heart of hearts, to get a quarter of a million dollars from some nut job who loves everything about the house and is willing to pay nearly double its market value. I am hoping to make a significant return on our investment and am willing to wait to hear what that is. But a couple houses in the neighborhood have recently sold in only a couple of days, like Stacey's, and they went for more than my imagination could grasp.

"What do you think about two-ten?" Bob asks. He clearly is starting low, but not too low to know his figure hasn't rounded the next big hump in the sixth-digit place. "Good return on your investment, sort of right in the middle of the comparables I looked up. Nice tag for a two-bedroom tract house, don't you think?"

Jenae is crushed.

"I think that's a good bit lower than we were thinking," I say.

"I want a quarter of a million dollars," Jenae says.

She isn't joking.

"All right," Bob says, "all right. I ain't hatin'. You tell me." He re-

minds us that we can put whatever price tag we want on it. We just
have to remember that a house priced too high can sour fast, no
matter how nice. "There's a house over on Thirteenth South," he
says, "by that fancy Liberty Heights grocer there — Liberty Heist,
am I right? — and that Japanese restaurant? The guy did a bunch
of junky work on it himself and he's asking for about fifty grand
too much. People won't even touch it. I show folks the place and
they like ask for those paper surgeon's booties to wear 'cause they
don't want the bad mojo on their soles, get it? All right. So. What
do you think?"

We push around some figures and begin to sweat, sitting at our
dining room table with Bob. We know he is right — we have seen
perfectly good houses in our neighborhood rot on the market for
months. They would cycle through different, increasingly pathetic
versions of their signs and agents until they ground down toward
entropic death and simply put up a For Sale by Owner sign in the
window — grim as a toe tag — like our own house when we bought
it. But we don't have a year or two to sell it, as Stanley did. We need
to get out in a couple of months and maybe turn a profit so we can
make a down payment on a house in Texas.

"Come on, guys," Bob says. "It's important, but it's not the secret
code to the reactor."

We look at each other and name a figure, splitting the difference
between Jenae's goal and Bob's initial proposal.

"Little high," Bob says, scratching his neck. He chips away at the
price until it feels both reasonably lofty and modest, we imagine,
to people who have dramatically better jobs than ours.

We agree.

"Sweet," Bob says. He claps and rubs his hands together like a
genie. "Here we go."

* * *

We have about three weeks to get things together before the sign goes in the yard. We are shooting for the weekend after Easter, right at the beginning of the season — three years almost to the day after Gram died. There is tons to do to get the house ready, but we have a timeline. I am in charge of finishing up work on the baseboards in the living and dining rooms, and Jenae is going to take care of the yard and the flower beds. She has already done a heroic job of planting the bulbs in the fall, while I was mired in job-search junk. She has planted more than a hundred tulips, dahlias, poppies, and irises, all according to a thoroughly planned flower map that she drew up. Some of the daffodils and tulips have already started to come up, but so have a lot of weeds. Bob has told us not to worry about the yard, though; he's going to send somebody over to clean the windows and take care of our lawn.

So while Jenae is at work, I get set to finish the baseboards. It isn't the kind of carpentry I know anything about — not that I know anything about any real carpentry — but this sort of work is what people actually see, and so, to a big extent, it matters.

It's a pretty tricky enterprise, I learn, to make a floor and a wall meet. Take the molding and baseboards. They exist to extend the foot of the wall cosmetically over the edge of the floor, like the hem of your pants. I suppose baseboards do other things — they look nice and give you an extra surface to paint and keep clean — but for the most part they're just window dressing, or in this case, floor dressing.

I am ashamed to admit that I so dreaded doing this last, relatively small task that we have lived in the house for almost three years without them. The varying width of the gaps was daunting but, as it turns out, easy to ignore. Until now.

The only solution is either to use crown molding on the floor — which would be, to say the least, unconventional — or to try some combination of baseboards and molding to layer the transition from the walls. This is all very pleasant to talk about, but when you're actually setting about making this manifest in the world, it becomes a little tricky. My job is essentially to build a picture frame for the floor, the problem being that neither room is square, and on top of that, I am going to have to build one frame and then another frame for that frame, including: two rooms with five doorways, a closet, three heat registers, four electrical outlets, a forty-five-degree slanted corner, a gently arched outer wall, and a floor that was laid at two different levels. I am not looking forward to this.

One afternoon, as I take measurement upon measurement, I stop for a break and notice, much to my surprise, men in our backyard. After a second of shock I realize it must be the crew that Bob was sending over, and suddenly I feel like quite the pimp. I not only have people working for me, I have somebody working for me who has other people working for me. Best yet, no cash comes out of my pocket. The house, our glorious house, is going to pay for them. I walk to the front and find that they have already been there.

The yard looks great, except for one thing: they have whacked down the flower beds along with the weeds.

I know I am going to have to tell Jenae before she sees it herself. "Hey, baby," I say, cuddling the phone by proxy. "You busy?"

"What's wrong?" she says. It is her mama bear voice. "Is Maggie all right?"

The worst time I had to make a call like this, we were living in our second-floor apartment in Columbus, using the fire escape as the main entrance. Maggie and I had just come back from our morning walk and were at the top of the rusty metal stairs when she spotted a squirrel on the first-floor roof. Maggie took off and jumped on it. The squirrel was long gone by the time Maggie hit the slate shingles and started to slide, slowly but inevitably, toward the edge. I practically jumped down the entire fire escape, but I wasn't able to beat her to the ground. She landed on all fours, wobbled for a second, and crumpled to her belly.

I picked her up as gently as I could and laid her across the back seat of my Jeep. When I started the engine, however, she sprang up in panic and struggled to get onto my lap. There is nothing, bar none, that Maggie hates more than the car.

After the vet gave her a miraculously clean bill of health, I called Jenae. (At that time, nobody except drug dealers and Don Johnson had cell phones, so I hadn't had a chance to call earlier.)

This is how I sound now, when I call to tell her about her flowers.

"No, baby," I say, "we're all safe and sound, and I think that's the important thing to remember here."

"What is it, then?" she says.

"The good news is the grass looks great."

When she gets home, she goes from sorrowful weeping to Old Testament keening. You would think that our own firstborn has been torn from her arms and smote with paving stones.

"Why don't you let me call Bob Plumb," I say. "I'm sure we can work something out. It was just a misunderstanding."

"No," she says. "No. I am going to call Bob Plumb."

I have to step outside.

Less than half an hour later, Bob pulls up in his white Acura to survey the damage. He is a pro.

"What a shame," he says. "All those flowers. All that *work.*"

Then he smiles his big Plumb smile. "How do we make this right?" he says. "I know there's no getting back your flowers or the work wasted, but how can we get close?"

Jenae looks as though she has just been asked to put a price on an orphanage fire.

"Do you want me to have my guys come back with a few flats of petunias or something? They can knock it out in a couple of minutes and you'll have a yard full of blooms before dark."

"No," Jenae says. "I want to do it. It's still my yard and I didn't spend hundreds of hours for a bunch of stupid petunias."

Bob looks at me generously. He is not judging me. He is not judging Jenae. This guy sells houses that are worth ten times what ours is. He knows this shit is stressful.

"How about this," Bob says. He reaches for his money clip and starts counting out twenties. "I know it's only getting close, right — I'm not paying you off — but would a hundred bucks help? Or a hundred fifty? Or no, I only got twenties. One-forty? Would that get you closer to where you want the yard to be?"

What could we say? He tucks the bills into Jenae's palm and pats her hand.

"I gotta go, kids," he says, maintaining eye contact but sidling back around to his car. "We'll be rolling soon and this will all be behind us. Don't sweat it."

Dragging myself around the house in a handyman's stations of the cross, I work toward the end of our seemingly perpetual list of projects. I lay the baseboards in the dining room with Liquid Nails à la Stanley, tack them in place with some tenpenny brads, and move on to the next room by lunchtime. The living room with its split-level floor is a lot more challenging, but I realize that because the difference in height is only a quarter of an inch, I can lay the baseboard on shims where there is a height difference, so it will be the same height all the way around. Then, when I go back to attach the quarter-round molding (basically a long wooden dowel about the size of a broomstick which has been sawed the long way into four equal pieces — take one of those and you've got a quarter of a round stick), it will cover the shims and the gap with only one Z-shaped joint, and nobody'll be the wiser. It is an obvious solution any tradesman would have known to do before he scratched his ass, but to me it was more complicated than French literary theories based on rhizomes.

That's not true. It is less complicated than rhizome theory, but it wouldn't have been an easy fix for anybody. This is a good fix not just anybody could have come up with. It's about damned time I stop apologizing for being decent at one or two things. I am going to get my PhD in a couple of weeks, and figuring out how to use a stick to cover a crack feels like the greater achievement.

The guys across the street moved into their place about the time we did ours, and as it turns out, they put their house on the market just a month before us. The house is no bigger than the cabin of a small crab boat, and the two men who live there, a husky, ruddy gay couple, could pass as fraternity brothers or missionaries.

One day while Jenae and I are replanting some decorative grasses in the parking strip, I talk with Marcus, the slightly bigger guy with the slightly darker goatee.

"It has been such a tremendous pain in the ass," he says. He sucks on his cigarette and exhales tensely. "For the first month," he says, "our realtor would call us three, four times a day and say, 'Can you guys be gone in half an hour?' So we'd have to split for an hour and drive around with our cat, because, you know, you can't trust any-body to not let little Brigham out. Weekdays, weekends, holidays . . . it never mattered. I'm just *so* tired. I just want it done."

We are standing across the street from each other. I'm holding a shovel like Pa Kettle and he's expertly smoking. I ask Marcus where they are moving.

"New development," he says, rolling his head and stroking his goatee. "Eagle Mountain. It's just north of Utah County. We'll have to play nice down there, but if we get what we're asking for out of this place, we can buy a brand-new house with three bed-rooms, a two-car garage, a yard, and a big flipping fence."

"Utah County?" I ask. Orem. Provo. Gilmore. Suicide mission, I think.

"I know, I know," he says. "But we work at eBay down there, and despite what the Church thinks, there's actually a lot of gay folks down that way. It'll be awesome. Anyway, I gotta go, but good luck with everything," he says. He flicks his cigarette down the street. "And my God, I hope you aren't asking too much. I don't want anybody to have to go through what we did for these months."

The big day, a Friday morning, comes with an eight A.M. call from Bob Plumb's brother, Rick. Bob told us that Rick is usually in-volved with most of the business, but he had broken his leg in a motocross accident and is getting fat back in the office eating all the fruit and cashews from the get-well baskets.

"Got some biters," Rick says. "Can we show it at one?"

"The sign's not even in the yard yet," I say.

"We have our ways," Rick says.

I say sure and flurry into action. I was hoping we'd at least get a good night's sleep, but the game isn't going to wait for me to hit my snooze button. As I brush my teeth, I wander around the house in a state of preemptive nostalgia, wondering if I am going to miss the underfoot feel of a fairly well-finished hardwood floor or the way the sun rises in the east over the Wasatch Mountains — ever so slightly visible through the one window if you stand, as I do, in my boxer shorts, brushing my teeth, gazing out.

Just then I notice a motorcycle parked out front. From time to time people would park their cars there to go to church events across the street, and occasionally sketchy guys in pimped-out Civics or Regals would swap some oregano or whatnot and then speed away. I called the cops a few times but never to any effect, though there seemed to be less commerce in the past year or so. Still, the motorcycle is disconcerting.

I continue to brush, and as I walk into the living room to open the curtains I find a guy standing on the corner, staring at our house. He is youngish, like me, and he is wearing a Colorado Avalanche jersey, talking on his cell phone. I blink. He waves. I close the curtains and go to the bathroom to spit.

Jenae is already at work, so I am left to fend for Maggie and Skillet while the realtors show the house. At first I think I'll drive around with the pets, but that's dumb. Maggie, of course, hates cars, and Skillet hates pretty much everything.

Not having any other options, I coax Skillet into his crate and put him in the back of my car. I urge Maggie to stay in the passenger seat while I start the engine, but before I have my seat belt buckled she leaps onto my lap.

It's a beautiful day. Spring is arguably what Utah does best. The snow has melted in the valley and the foothills, so there is plenty of runoff to spruce up the lawns and gardens. Everywhere trees bud forth and flowers burst like hormonal teenagers. I play Maggie's favorite Iron & Wine album on the stereo, figuring we have an hour to kill. Skillet begins his air-raid-siren yowling from the back, and as we pass a park on McClelland all the parents look up warily at the noise. Even from the street it must sound as if I am giving the little jerk the Gitmo treatment. I suppose I am, but Maggie is getting more and more frantic on my lap, and her stomach is throbbing and wrenching as though she has swallowed a couple of gyroscopes.

What the hell, I think, I'll take them to Sugarhouse Park.

The night before, there was a story on the news about a little girl who was playing near the river in the park and got swept away by the high water. There happened to be a Boy Scout downriver (and even though this is Salt Lake City, you can't take for granted that there will be one posted every fifty feet). If he hadn't been there, she'd have been a goner. As it was, she got sucked through a forty-foot culvert that ran under the park road. She was lucky that no grating covered the culvert or she would have been blasted into it like so much sausage through a grinder's die.

I would take Maggie to Sugarhouse Park late in the summer, when the water was so calm she could jump in and lie in the sandy shallows. The river is fed entirely by snowmelt, so even in July and August the water is nut-wrenchingly cold. I figured we would hang out on the park's ridge on 17th East, which overlooks the rest of the valley. Today there are a few sunbathers braving the mid-fifties temperature, folks playing fetch with their dogs, and a few teenagers who must be ditching class from Highland High School next door. I get Skillet out and put him a few yards away under an apple tree and then release Maggie. She bounds out of the car and springs through the shaggy grass like a puppy, leaving the anxiety of the car behind along with all of the shed fur now coating my lap. Then she realizes that Skillet's still with us and is immediately bummed out.

She casts a doubtful expression my way. I grab a tennis ball and chuck it down the hill. The ball bounces and rolls until it's damn near in the river. I can hear the water from two hundred yards away. It must be running really hard and high. Maggie sprints after the ball, and when she scoops it up like a sparrow she keeps running, almost out of control, the hill is so steep. I start to scream because she is too close to the water, but in a smooth pivot she pulls easily out of her descent and heads back uphill to me and her orange bastard brother.

I throw the ball more carefully now, but I know this can't last long. She is a spaniel, bred to hunt. All her life she has insisted on staying close to me whenever we were in a park. If I stopped walking, she stopped walking. It was a little disappointing at first; most dog owners have fanciful dreams of taking their pooches to the park on a Saturday morning with a newspaper and a cup of coffee and kicking back on a bench while their doggies perform perfect circuits of joy like furry satellites. Not my Maggie. If I sit on a park bench, she wants to sit next to me, preferably on the bench.

What the hell, I figure. I open Skillet's crate carefully, fearing he'll be a cat-in-the-box and erupt from his blue plastic cell and rocket down the hill. I swing open the gate but he doesn't budge. Despite the fact that the inside of his crate is featureless and smooth, he has managed to adhere himself to the interior.

As I drag him out and put his fat-boy harness on, I look around through his eyes and see that the circumference of his known world has just expanded from 1,700 or so square feet (plus a small fenced-in backyard) to—what?—a few hundred square miles, including the tectonic drama of the Wasatch Mountains behind us, the Oquirrh Mountains across the valley, all of metro Salt Lake City, and the great saline pond itself, glinting in the distance. It must feel as if the world has been a child's shoebox diorama and, without warning, the roof and walls fall away to reveal that your little hut has been jettisoned into nearly infinite space.

Once I get him all suited up, I don't want to leave anything behind. There is no telling how far and wide Skillet might like to wander. I have him on one of those cheap retractable leashes, and I think he might really like it. We head down the hill, Skillet sulkily in tow, Maggie bounding in all her spaniel glory.

Everything is on the line. How the next few days or weeks turn out will by and large determine how well we have done with the house. If we priced it too high and the work we did inside was deemed too quirky or shoddy, we'll be sitting on an inert stack of bricks and sticks, desperate for a buyer, unless some bank or turn-and-burn investor takes it over for pennies on the dollar. It seems that all our neighbors are selling their houses within a couple of days — or not at all.

My phone rings as we head down toward the river. The water is running so loudly that I can barely hear Rick Plumb.

"Now we're cooking, baby," he says. "Got room at the dance for a couple more?"

Maggie frolics ahead of me and Skillet is lumped in place behind, refusing to move.

"Sweet," I say to Rick, without enthusiasm. This means I am going to have to do something with the pets for another hour at least. Sounds like no big deal, but there's a reason you see only weird, depraved people with cats on leashes.

The next day comes and no offer follows. We can hardly complain — it is only the second day — but still. More showings are scheduled, however, and though it is a little tedious, we decide to follow the same routine. Jenae has to work, and there are folks lined up to see the house all morning and afternoon, so I hope that the critters can settle down in the park with me for a lazy day.

I'm carrying the messenger bag that our dear friend Melanie has recently given me upon completion of my degree. It's a classic black bag that's small enough to take anywhere but big enough for all the essentials: wallet, phone, keys, cinnamon-raisin bagel (untoasted, plain cream cheese), book (*Another Bullshit Night in Suck City*), and a few poop bags for, you know, whomever. Carrying everything I need makes me feel jaunty and adventurous, like a latter-day Marquette — only my Joliet is furry and English, not French, and we have a grossly obese orange-and-white hairball in lieu of a foxy Indian guide.

Before we hunker down for the morning, Maggie leads Skillet and me into the woods by the river, and the thought that this house selling is going to take not days but weeks — maybe months, God help us — begins to sink in. This is only the second day in the park with the dog and cat together, and it is kind of fun, but I have serious doubts about doing it another, say, thirty or forty times. It's beginning to look as if taking ten or fifteen grand off the price might well be worth it.

The fast water is at once soothing and frightening. Skillet wants nothing to do with it, and Maggie, I assume, will know to do the same. I, however, love being near it. The rush and the thunder of it is nothing like the gentle flow in late summer. Whereas in August it seems as calm as a birdbath, the river is now a good five or six feet deep and runs with the force of what it is: nature shedding its winter weight down the side of a mountain and into a narrow-shouldered channel. It's violently gorgeous.

From a high bank, Maggie sniffs at the water. In the summer, she usually can't even see the river from here. Now it is right at her nose.

"Bunny," I say firmly. "Too cold, too fast. No fun for rabbits."

Maggie scoots backward and resumes wagging and sniffing in the tall weeds around the riverbank. Skillet is over it. Rare is the occasion when a cat wants nothing more than to get back into his own crate, but this is one of those times. I just want to give Maggie a little more adventure time before we return to our pensive perch atop the hill, waiting for the brothers Plumb to call and let us back into our home.

Across the river, a band of people marches in some kind of procession. The road flows through the park at that point in a sharp bend around a hill, and the parade wends upward. There aren't many marchers, and they don't look overly organized or politically motivated. It's more of a *They're Flip-Flops, Not Thongs!* walk than a radical demonstration, I decide. Then again, I can't hear a peep over the rushing river. For all I know, they could have Wagner raging over loudspeakers in preparation for a march on Idaho.

Out of the corner of my eye, I notice a Latino man deeper in the woods, downstream from us. He wears mirrored sunglasses and a long braid and leans against Highland High's fence. He reminds me of a cross between Carlos Santana and Jesus. He doesn't pay any attention to me, but I know he knows I am here. He just gazes through the trees at the people across the river.

I watch the parade for a few more seconds to see if I can figure out what it is that holds this guy's attention. I hope it won't involve a sniper rifle, say, or petroleum jelly.

I decide it's best to give the dude a wide berth, so instead of following the high path that leads by the school fence, we can skirt around through the brush by the river. But Skillet is protesting, doing his best to turn himself into a concrete goose, and as I drag him down the tangled path, I look up just in time to see Maggie test the river with her paw.

I wasn't thinking. This is, after all, the part of the river where, in the summer, I would let her swim. No wonder she wouldn't go in the upper part; the water was almost always too fast there. But by this point it has usually calmed down. Certainly by July. But today it's fast and bad as a flash flood in a slot canyon, where ranchers sometimes lose entire herds of cattle.

I scream at Maggie as loudly and forcefully as I can, but I'm not sure she can hear me over the roar of the river. She turns around, but in doing so steps in the water, and all at once she is afloat and begins bobbing and spinning away in the current. I run toward her but the eddy in which she swirls immediately whorls into the rest of the fast water, and just as I reach the river's edge the water sucks her downstream faster than I could swim after her.

"Skillet!" I shout, though he has never heeded a word I say. I yell one more time and yank him down the path, but he dives for a bush and jerks himself out of the harness and I'm left holding an empty leash. Both of my babies are in the wind.

There is no time to think or feel or worry or plan. I just know that in a heartbeat I went from being a proud daddy of two sweet critters to a man faced with the decision of letting one go for the sake of keeping the other safe, or risking the lives of both in an attempt to retrieve the first.

I think of that little girl who was swept downstream two days ago and the scout who himself could have easily drowned and the culvert she was sucked under and all that water and all those rocks, and decide it is simply time to act. I look at the Latino guy but see only my panicked reflection in his glasses.

I plow through the brush downstream to where I know there is, at least in the latter part of summer, a decent crossing. I dive through the branches and bushes and manage to get to the clearing just ahead of Maggie. The river is still high and fast, and I know if I don't go in ahead of her there is no way I can get her out.

I think of Jenae and how, without her knowledge, all her loved ones are going to be thrown in a river with no real promise of escape. I think of my mom and how unlikely it is that she could survive the piling on of another death so close to the anniversary of her own mom's passing. I pause only for the hint of a prayer, because as unsafe as I know that water is, there's no way I can slink back home with empty, dry arms.

I imagine Skillet might have tried to follow me through the brush or might have done what he has been doing all day: following Maggie. I'll have precious little chance of catching him, I know, but if I don't hurry, Maggie is going to sweep past me and away for good, so in I jump, and the shock and rush of all that cold, fast water hits my body all at once, as if the river is a frigid, liquid form of electricity.

Maggie rushes into view, struggling to keep her head above water, paddling fiercely but with little hope of getting to shore on her own. I didn't even think about how deep the river would be for me — I never imagined it'd be up to my head — and a surge of water blows my sunglasses off my face and fills my messenger bag like a lead parachute. The water plumes up my body and face, eddying turbulently behind me. I lean into the stream as if I am trying to dam the river itself. I tilt just an inch too far, though, and for a second I can't touch bottom. I rudder myself back to something approaching vertical just in time, and there is Maggie coming at me like a fast and furry tugboat. I open my arms and she hits me square in the chest.

I hold on tight, and water rushes into my mouth and lungs, and it is so, so cold. I can't believe that only moments ago I was almost hot and contemplating sunbathing, and here we are, fighting for our lives in the middle of a freezing river: a boy and his dog and maybe his damned cat to boot.

But there is no time to wait for Skillet. If he is in that water, he's as good as gone. With Maggie in my arms, I can't even get back to the bank we came from. It's only five feet away, but the river is too strong and cold and I am coughing up froth and struggling to keep Maggie against my chest — I don't know what will happen if I take another lungful of water. It's not that I think I will drown, but one good knock on the noggin or neck and what else would it take to make things catastrophic? I try to let the river guide me into the bank, and sweet Melanie's messenger bag acts something like a keel, keeping me more or less square so that I can hold Maggie tight and not head too fast, spaniel-first, for some tree trunk or rock. We pass a snag of roots and brush and I grab onto whatever I can, afraid it is the only chance we are getting, and I roughly shove Maggie ashore.

I worry that she might have been hurt, maybe badly, but she gets herself upright immediately and shakes her coat off as though preparing for another swim. I am so relieved I almost fail to realize that I haven't yet managed to get myself out of the river. I pull hard on the roots and paw myself to shore.

"Come on, bunny," I yell to Maggie. There is no time to check for injuries — we have to get back to the other side. I am freezing and hacking up water, but we run as fast as our numb little limbs can carry us. I feel the stares of some paraders and a few kids playing basketball up ahead by the bridge. We must look quite a sight. Here it is, sunny and in the fifties, and along comes a profoundly soggy dog and her dad, water sloshing out of his bag.

I am so happy that Maggie sailed right into my arms, that she seems blithely childlike and ready to go on her next big adventure, not having any idea how close a call she — we — really had. But there is no time to relax. My lungs are bursting with icy water and my throat aches from screaming and water squishes out of my shoes and the pockets of my jeans. I can barely see through the brush at the base of the river and can't spot Skillet anywhere. I can't say that I ever felt anything like affection for the little putz, but I know in some strange way he makes Jenae happy, and there is neither rhetoric nor apology enough to explain how I have managed to save my dog but not her cat.

The bridge is broad and solid, with a cement walkway and steel railings painted purple, and it is the only way to get to the other side of the river within a mile. Once across, I stop and look up to find Jesus still gazing across the river with his mirrored sunglasses.

"Where's Skillet?" I ask Jesus. I gesture around the woods, surprised to find I am still holding the retractable leash with his empty fat-boy harness dangling there.

I know I'm not making any sense, asking this guy for a frying pan, for all he knows, but I can't do any better. I am frantic and bewildered and don't know which way to turn.

But Jesus knows. Without a word, he raises his right arm and points downstream.

I scan the riverbank, calling out "*Kitty kitty kitty,*" because that's what you're supposed to do when you lose a cat, despite the fact that my cat has only ever heard me call him Skillet, Drillbit, Harelip, McGarret (from *Hawaii Five-o,* which he and Jenae love), Snakebit, Rarebit, or Fat Boy. His wide orange-and-white hide should be easy to see — unless he's in the water.

And then, hunkering just about where he was when I yanked him out of his harness, trying to hide from the great wide world under a shrub, there he is. Little thug.

I scoop him up and hold him tight against my chest. He immediately claws at me, because I am soaked to the bone and still dripping cold water and it is probably the second-biggest shock of his day, but I won't let him go for anything. Maggie and Skillet and I wave to Jesus and slosh back the strange way we have come.

We plop down in a clearing beneath some pine trees and try to catch our breath. I strip off as much as I decently can and spread out my clothes and the contents of my bag to dry on the grass. I haven't lost anything, but the book I brought is bloated to three times its original size and all I can get my cell phone to do is gurgle. I wait as long as I can, and after dragging the wet, recalcitrant pets across the vast steppe of Sugarhouse Park to the car, and driving home, I find, thankfully, no one. I want to call the Plumb brothers, but I only had their number stored in my cell phone. Before I hop in the shower, I give both the animals as much cat food as they can eat (yes, Maggie too) and call Jenae.

"So everybody's fine," I say.

"Oh, my God, what happened?" she says. She knows it isn't going to be about flowers this time. "Maggie? Skillet?"

"Remember that bit on the news?" I say. I pace around the kitchen floor, leaving soggy footprints on the slate. "The part about the water being high in Sugarhouse Park?"

"Oh, my God. You did not."

"Well," I say, "we did, and it was, but everybody's all right."

"Oh," she says again. "My God. I would have *killed* you if you drowned."

As I warm up in the shower, I begin to feel achy and emotional. The hot water washing over me in my house is such a merciful respite, it's hard to believe it comes from the same source as all that snowmelt that coursed over my body an hour ago. But there isn't time to relax. There might be another showing any minute, and though I don't really care that much about it given the events of my morning, I don't want to have to explain it to a nice young preapproved couple and their realtor.

Just as I am drying off, the phone rings.

"Bob says no more water." It's Jenae. I think she means the shower and begin to remind her that it is a low-flow showerhead and it was a traumatic morning — then I get it. "He said that people die in that river — he grew up here in Sugarhouse, remember? — and don't be a dumbass, stay out of it. That, and there are no more showings today."

I am relieved. I am disappointed. I am absolutely wiped out.

That evening, I spread our scratchy blue-plaid blanket on the grass and we all hang out in the backyard, trying to relish the remaining days in our little Sugarhouse home. Nicole and Erik, their new baby girl Zoë, and Cleo their monster dog come over. We grill brats and corn on the cob, drink wine, tickle the baby, and watch Skillet abuse a dog ten times his size. It's hard to imagine we are ever going to leave this place.

The next morning, Sunday, Rick Plumb calls at eight and says that somebody who has already seen the house wants to come by again.

"I know it's a pain in the ass," he says. I imagine him with his cast-covered leg propped on an open drawer, eating grapes by the pound. "And I know it's Sunday, but he said you don't have to leave if you don't want to. I kinda hinted that it might be inconvenient, but Bob said not to hate on 'em. You only need one buyer."

Point made.

In an hour the guy in the Avalanche jersey shows up, this time with his girlfriend and his own agent. His name is Brian and he's a systems guy — whatever that means — for a mining company, and he says he just had to see the place again.

"Stay, stay," Brian urges us as we begin to pack up the critters. "Really. I just want to show my girlfriend."

We don't quite know where to be or how much to act like what is obviously true: we own the place and hope to make a lot of money from it.

Brian takes his tank-topped, flip-flopped girlfriend around while their agent hangs back and strokes his mustache like a Bond villain petting his lap dog.

"Seems like a nice place," he says. "Nice neighborhood. I like nice neighborhoods."

"Yep," I say. "Me too." I wish Bob Plumb were here for this. He has warned us about direct contact with buyers and other agents.

"Price is a little much," Brian says, staring critically at the soffits. "A little much, don't you think?"

I look at him. Twenty-four hours ago I was in danger of drowning. "It's what we're asking," I say.

"Hey, okay, kemosabe," he says, holding his hands up. "Your house, your price."

Brian and his girlfriend join us outside. If she is enamored with the place, she doesn't show it. Brian, on the other hand, glows as though he has gotten into Jenae's buffing cream.

"I just love it," he says, rushing us to shake our hands. "It's such a great house."

His agent rolls his eyes.

"He can't stop talking about all the stainless stuff in the kitchen," his girlfriend says.

"And the slate," Brian says. "That is slate, right? And the countertop. What is that? Concrete? I can't believe it. I *love* it."

We thank him and watch his agent glower.

"Are you guys going to be around later," Brian says, "like this afternoon?"

"You bet," I say. "We might go for a little swim, but beyond that, we'll be here."

Jenae pokes me hard in the ribs and leaves her finger there to let me know I am not funny, not even a little.

Homecoming

✳ ✳ ✳

THE PLAN WAS to try to relax and live as if Texas were home. Our house payments were lower than the cheapest rent I'd ever paid; they called deep-fried tortillas smothered in nacho cheese "salad"; and Bruce was only a couple of hours away and visited every few weeks to make sure the shoe-size cockroaches hadn't carried us or any of our unopened beer off into the piney woods for good. Yet it was a long way from the place I called home, and I wound up getting a shot at a job up north.

We went to Nebraska for Christmas, and to Wisconsin for New Year's, right before my job interview in Minnesota. My mom was still negotiating life with her two Bobs. Ever since her husband fairly appraised Grandpa's grilled tilapia as "a little over-done" — the single dish he prepared every time he cooked, which he did by setting it on fire and letting it burn itself out — Grandpa refused to share any space with Bob. So our plan was to have dinners with Bob and lunches with Grandpa.

On New Year's Day, we struggled to decide on a restaurant Grandpa didn't associate with Tonya, who had in the meantime remarried Tim, so we picked a place equally objectionable to all of us: the Champps sports bar in Brookfield. The place was packed with Badger fans wearing red-and-white pelts and oversize wedges of plastic cheddar on their heads.

"I'm not sure I'm up for this," Jenae said. It had hardly been a rockin' New Year's Eve the night before. We had all gone to bed before the ball dropped. "I feel a little . . . thick," she said.

A grim hostess with glasses in the shape of the year showed us to our table. Grandpa was slower than ever today, glum about Tonya's remarriage, so when we finally got installed in our booth I ordered a round of bloody marys — in Wisconsin they come with a beer chaser, a stick of beef jerky, and every other medicinal garnish they've got at the bar — and I thought everybody would be on the mend inside a couple of minutes.

Instead, Jenae struggled to keep her burger from talking back, while Grandpa sat resentfully quiet because he couldn't hear over the din of the football game, which was being broadcast on every flat surface in the bar, and my mom dealt with her predeparture depression, knowing that she wasn't going to see us for a while — unless things went really right at the interview. Everybody was just kind of out of it.

When we got back to Grandpa's apartment building, we left the girls in the car while I shuffled with him to his unit. "You know, Matt," he said, "I've been thinking about what you do, with your writing and all?"

"Yeah?" I said. He knew I wrote short stories and essays that weren't very appealing to him compared to the subtle ghost/spy/romance/thrillers he'd lately been checking out of the library by the bushel.

"Yeah," he said. "And I've got an idea for you. For a book."

"Is that right?" I said as we arrived at his door.

"It is," he said. He glanced at me, still a wink of trouble left in him. "And it would be pretty racy stuff, let me tell you what. But

I don't expect you're interested in writing something like that. Something that would involve, say, a gentleman, a hot young lady, and some trouble."

"We'll see," I told him, giving him one last hug. "I just might."

By the time we got back to my mom's condo, we were all ready for a cocktail — except Jenae. She just wanted to head upstairs to crash, she said. She was so tired she couldn't think of eating or drinking anything else today.

"Not even cottage cheese?" I said, tucking her in.

"I hate you," Jenae said. "Don't make me hurt your face parts."

I kissed her on the forehead and went downstairs.

My mom and Bob were sitting in their easy chairs, and I told them about Jenae, hoping they wouldn't be too sore about her absence.

"What," Bob said, hoisting his half brandy, half crème de menthe, "is she *prejke?*"

I didn't know if the word was Czech or Polish or what, but I knew what he meant, and in my gut I knew he was right.

"Oh, Bob," my mom said, blushing, embarrassed but hopeful. "Goodness gracious."

My watch says it's eight and a half months later, and now we live in Minnesota, waiting for our little package to be delivered any minute. Even though she's about six hours away, my mom is so relieved we've come, more or less, home.

We're tucked in a little house half a block from a small lake, but in trade for its great location, the place needs a little TLC. We looked at houses that were readier to go, eighty-six of them to be exact, but none nearly as close to a place for Maggie and our muffin-in-the-oven to romp and run. There's so much more to say, but now that the drywall's finally hung, taped, sanded, and prepped, it's time to finish tiling the bathroom before our sarcastic plumber comes back to install the "sophisticated" toilet Jenae picked out, and by then the primer I threw on the walls upstairs this morning should be dry enough so we can paint what will be our bedroom — and, of course, the biscuit-cute dormered room that will be the nursery for we know not who but are sure going to find out soon.

Acknowledgments

I would like to thank all of the people without whom this book would not have been possible: Jim Rutman, my agent nonpareil, and his outstanding assistant, Adelaide Wainright; Larry Cooper, my supremely kind and patient manuscript editor; and everyone at HMH, but especially Adrienne Brodeur, my resplendent editor. I will need to learn several new languages to adequately thank you.

My heartfelt gratitude goes to all my teachers, but foremost: Robin Hemley, Bill Roorbach, Lee K. Abbott, Paisley Rekdal, and the beatific Melanie Rae Thon.

To all my classmates, my deepest thanks. From The Ohio State University: Mike Løhre, Kirk Robinson, Dan O'Dair, Tom Moss, Juliet Williams, Mark Steinwachs, and Bryan Narendorf. From the University of Utah: Nicole Walker, Erik Sather, Pamela Balluck, Steve Lehigh, Julie Pagel, Steve Tuttle, and Susan Goslee.

I am greatly indebted to my colleagues near and far who have helped in myriad ways: Christine Butterworth-McDermott, John McDermott, Matt Ramsey, Mike Martin, Lon Otto, Leslie Adrienne Miller, J. C. Hallman, Todd Lawrence, Andy Scheiber, Liz Wilkinson, and Ray MacKenzie.

This book would not have been completed without the generous and kind support of the National Endowment for the Arts. I also want to thank Michelle Wildgen at *Tin House* and Michael Cyznejewski at *Mid-American Review*.

To Jacob Paul, my dear friend who has literally saved my life more than once, not to mention been a patient and stupendous reader of several drafts of this book; suffice it to say, I owe you.

To Bruce Machart, and to sweet Marya, and to Bruce's dear parents, Allen and Bobbie Gay, well . . . where am I gonna find enough thanks to put on your table? In many ways, this book wouldn't exist without you, your literary mentorship, and your inestimable friendship.

I could not have done any of this without the support and encouragement of my grandparents, Jeanne and Robert Tucker, and their wondrous daughter, my mother, my hero, Patti Ann.

Jenae, it's going to take me a lifetime to thank you. Allow me to begin by saying simply this: I may have written this book, but you are its ink, its white space, its binding, its cover. Tell Emory, *You're the names of things*.